Quarterly Essay

Quarterly Essay is published four times a year by Black Inc., an imprint of Schwartz Books Pty Ltd. Publisher: Morry Schwartz.

ISBN 9781760644239 ISSN 1444-884x

Subscriptions – 1 year print & digital (4 issues): $89.99 within Australia incl. GST. Outside Australia $124.99. 2 years print & digital (8 issues): $169.99 within Australia incl. GST. 1 year digital only: $59.99.

Payment may be made by Mastercard or Visa, or by cheque made out to Schwartz Books. Payment includes postage and handling.

To subscribe, fill out and post the subscription card or form inside this issue, or subscribe online:

quarterlyessay.com
subscribe@quarterlyessay.com
Phone: 61 3 9486 0288

Correspondence should be addressed to:

The Editor, Quarterly Essay
22–24 Northumberland Street
Collingwood VIC 3066 Australia
Phone: 61 3 9486 0288 / Fax: 61 3 9011 6106
Email: quarterlyessay@blackincbooks.com

Editor: Chris Feik. Management: Elisabeth Young. Publicity: Anna Lensky. Design: Guy Mirabella. Associate Editor: Kirstie Innes-Will. Production Coordinator: Marilyn de Castro. Typesetting: Typography Studio. Figures by Alan Laver.

Printed in Australia by McPherson's Printing Group. The paper used to produce this book comes from wood grown in sustainable forests.

THE GREAT DIVIDE

Australia's housing mess and how to fix it

Alan Kohler

THREE GENERATIONS OF HOUSING

My parents were married in 1951 and, with a war service loan, bought a block of land in South Oakleigh, eight miles from Melbourne's CBD. I don't know what my dad was making then, but he was a carpenter and apparently the average wage of a carpenter in 1951 was about 80 shillings a week, or £350 a year. And judging by average prices back then, they would have paid about £1000 for the land. (By the way, the median house price had more than doubled in 1950, recovering the big fall caused by price controls during World War II, on which more later.)

Dad built the house himself, including making the bricks, working on weekends and at night, and Mum and Dad lived in a garage, to which I was brought home when I was born and where I spent the first three years of my life. But if they had bought a house and land package, which was rather more common than building it yourself, they would have paid around £1250. So, like the median family at the time, they would have paid about 3.5 times household income (Mum didn't work) for their first house, which was about average for the time.

When my wife and I bought our first house, in 1980, we paid roughly the median house price of $40,000, and I was making around the average weekly earnings as a young journalist – $220 a week, or $11,500 a year. So we also paid about 3.5 times my salary for the house, although we were better off than my parents because my wife was working, for about the same salary as mine, and my mum didn't, which was normal for both times. Workforce participation for thirty-year-old women had increased from 32 to 50 per cent by 1980, as a result of the social/sexual revolution of the 1960s and '70s.

Over the past four years, our three children and their partners all bought their own first houses. They're doing it later than we did, and much later than my parents, so they're making better money, and both partners are working, of course, but they paid about 7.5 times each income for their houses. That was typical: in August 2023, the median Australian house price was $732,886, which was 7.4 times annualised average weekly earnings.

In other words, my children – and all young people today – are paying more than twice the multiple of their income for a house than their parents – and their grandparents – did, and it's only vaguely possible because both partners work to pay it off.

What happened, and when it happened, is evident in Figures 1 and 2.

The problem started with the new millennium.

It is impossible to overstate the significance to Australian society of what happened then. The shift that began around 2000 in the relationship between the cost of housing and both average incomes and the rest of the economy has altered everything about the way Australia operates and Australians live.

Six per cent compound annual growth in the value of houses over the past twenty-three years versus 3 per cent annual growth in average incomes has meant that household debt has had to increase from half to twice average disposable income, and from 40 per cent of GDP to 120 per cent. This is the most important single fact about the Australian economy. The large amount of housing debt Australians carry means that interest rates have a much greater impact on their lives, and this in turn affects inflation, wages, employment and economic growth. In the Australian economy, the price of houses is not everything, but it's almost everything, as economist Paul Krugman once said of productivity.

Figure 1 House prices and wages (full-time weekly earnings, index: 1970 = 100)

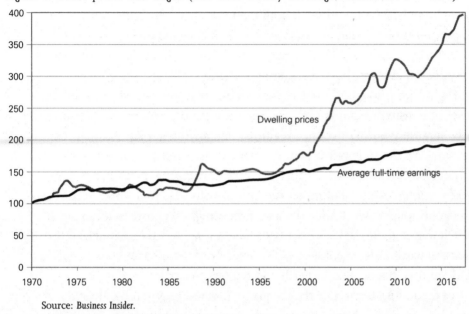

Source: *Business Insider.*

Figure 2 House price / GDP per capita

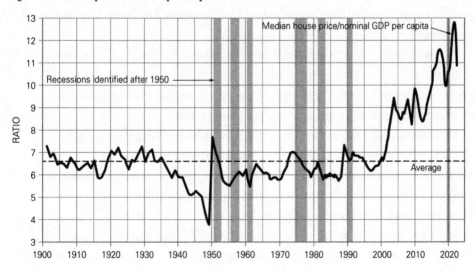

Source: *Minack Advisers.*

Land and energy are the two basic economic inputs apart from labour, but while Australia has more of both than just about any other country, we export most of the energy and price our own at global parity, so there's no home-grown advantage there, and we crowd into a few cities and pay each other seven to eight times our salaries for land.

High-priced houses do not create wealth; they redistribute it. And the level of housing wealth is both meaningless and destructive. It's meaningless because we can't use the wealth to buy anything else – a yacht or a fast car. We can only buy other expensive houses: sell your house and you have to buy another one, cheaper if you're downsizing, more expensive if you're still growing a family. At the end of your life, your children get to use your housing wealth for their own housing, except we're all living so much longer these days it's usually too late to be useful. And much of this housing wealth is concentrated in Sydney, where the median house value is $1.1 million, double that of Perth and regional Australia.

It's destructive because of the inequality that results: with so much wealth concentrated in the home, it stays with those who already own a house and within their families. For someone with little or no family housing equity behind them, it's virtually impossible to break out of the cycle and build new wealth.

As I will argue, it will be impossible to return the price of housing to something less destructive – preferably to what it was when my parents and I bought our first houses – without purging the idea that housing is a means to create wealth as opposed to simply a place to live.

That's easier said than done, as China's president, Xi Jinping, has found. He's been banging on about this for five years, saying that housing is not for speculation but for living in, but no one seems to be listening in China, and no one would be listening here either if the prime minister was saying the same thing. But anyway, he's not.

The growth in the value of Australian land has fundamentally changed society, in two ways. First, generations of young Australians are being held back financially by the cost of shelter, especially if they live somewhere near a CBD and especially in Sydney or Melbourne; and second, the way wealth is generated has changed. Education and hard work are no longer the main determinants of how wealthy you are; now it comes down to where you live and what sort of house you inherit from your parents.

It means Australia is less of an egalitarian meritocracy. Material success is now largely a function of geography, not accomplishment. Moreover, the geographic wealth gap is being widened by climate change, as floods and bushfires make living in large parts of the country uninsurable and financially crippling, but many families have no choice but to stay where they are because those areas are low-priced and they can't afford to move.

The houses we live in, the places we call home and bring up our families in, have been turned into speculative investment assets by the fifty years of government policy failure, financialisation and greed that resulted in twenty-five years of exploding house prices. The doubling of prices as a proportion of both average income and GDP per capita has turned a house from somewhere to live while you get on with the rest of your life into the main thing, and for many people a terrible burden.

The problem of housing affordability now dominates the national consciousness and has affected the lives of everyone, dividing Australia into those who own a house and those who don't; those whose families have housing wealth to pass on and those who don't. And what's more, most people now believe that the way to build wealth is to buy a house, and then another one, and another one after that, or to keep upgrading the one you live in. Or both.

A home is no longer what Australia's longest-serving prime minister, Robert Menzies, who championed home ownership and what he called "little capitalists," once extolled: "One of the best instincts in us is that which induces us to have one little piece of earth with a house and a garden which is ours; to which we can withdraw, in which we can be among our friends, into which no stranger may come against our will."

There have been many fine words spoken before and after Menzies by both well-meaning and cynical politicians, but the political class as a whole has failed Australians at all levels – federal, state and local government – for a simple reason that former prime minister John Howard once put into words: "No one ever came up to me to complain about the increase in the value of their home." Howard did more than anyone to make housing unaffordable, but at least he was honest about why.

In my view, the quiet political conspiracy identified by Howard to preserve and increase the value of houses to keep the majority of voters happy has been amplified by the banks doing the same thing to increase their profits. Australia is in the grip of a "bankocracy," in which four banks control our access to money. Their profits, and therefore the salaries of their executives, depend on both the volume and the value of their assets growing.

The volume of their assets (that is, the number of loans) increases because Australians believe the only way to increase their wealth is to borrow 80 to 100 per cent of the value of one or more houses; and the value grows because the banks' customers compete with each other to buy the houses and push up their prices and therefore the size of their loans. The more house prices rise, the greater the banks' profits. As US investment guru Charlie Munger says: "Show me the incentive and I'll show you the outcome."

The way real estate works in Australia is that the federal government and banks encourage demand for it and state and local governments restrict the supply of it. The states restrict supply through zoning, and local councils do it by their planning decisions every day. Federal government decisions increase demand for housing in four main ways: first, through interest rates; second, with immigration; third, with tax breaks for investors and home owners; and fourth, with grants to first home buyers.

In recent years, interest rates have been the main thing determining house prices, although they are not controlled by federal politicians but rather by the independent Reserve Bank of Australia. It is a federal body, appointed by the treasurer, and it manages the economy mainly through housing. That is, interest rates regulate the cost of housing and therefore the demand for it, and to a lesser extent the supply. By reducing or increasing the cost of shelter, the RBA controls our spending on everything else, which in turn governs the level of employment and inflation.

Incidentally, the result of the thing called monetary policy is that borrowers bear the entire burden of economic adjustment. And not just all borrowers – it's the ones who are already living on the edge. Rich borrowers are fine – they've got plenty left after higher repayments, so their spending doesn't change and they don't contribute to the economic adjustment. The spending cuts that result in slower economic growth are entirely made by those who are already struggling to make ends meet: the use of housing to regulate the economy is essentially a policy of cruelty.

As I will explain in more detail later, three main things pushed up demand for housing after 2000: a sharp lift in immigration that increased the number of people needing a place to live; capital gains tax breaks and negative gearing, which represent a $96 billion per year subsidy for buying houses; and federal first home buyer grants, which represent a $1.5 billion direct addition to house prices each year.

As for supply, in 2018, researchers at the RBA figured out that zoning restrictions raised the average price of detached houses by 73 per cent in Sydney, 69 per cent in Melbourne and 29 per cent in Brisbane. For apartments, the figures were 85 per cent in Sydney, 30 per cent in Melbourne and 26 per cent in Brisbane. Those are astonishing numbers, and that's without including the effect of local government planning decisions, which are, by definition, haphazard and unquantifiable but mostly aimed at keeping local councillors in a job by keeping the existing residents happy by making sure they don't let in too many new ones.

As Figure 3 shows, house prices started trending higher for the first time after World War II, but up to the turn of the millennium they were more or less keeping pace with incomes and the size of the economy.

At the same time as everybody was worrying about the world's computers grinding to a halt with Y2K, there was a collision between demand and supply and house prices started to depart from the rest of the economy, and from our incomes. What happened in the year 2000? Well, that's what

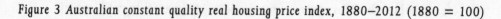

Figure 3 *Australian constant quality real housing price index, 1880–2012 (1880 = 100)*

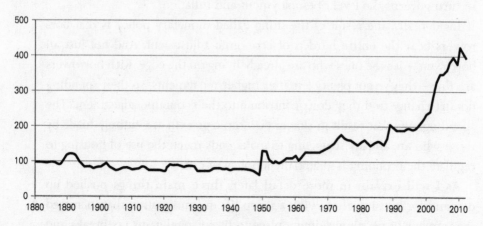

Source: Philip Soos, using data from ABS, Stapledon.

this Quarterly Essay is about; as I'll explain, the nitro of a surge in demand around that time mixed with the existing glycerine of restricted supply to create an explosion that has blown up the Australia that our parents knew.

And each of those things was almost entirely due to government policies, either the unintended consequences of misguided ideas or deliberate policies designed to preserve the wealth of the majority of voters – that is, those who own a house. If governments caused the problem, can governments fix it? Theoretically yes, but it's politically easier to make an asset worth more than to make it worth less. As I'll explain in the final chapter, actually doing something about housing affordability would require courage, Minister.

THE NUMBERS

Up to the turn of the millennium, the cost of a place to live basically kept up with the growth in both incomes and the economy. When the new millennium got underway, everything changed.

And the big losers from what has happened are those born after 1983 – the millennials who were just becoming adults when they grew into their generational label in 2000 at the same time house prices started taking off. And unless something is done about it, every generation after them, including the millennials' own children, will be even bigger losers because house prices have kept rising to this day, and will keep rising faster than incomes.

"Mortgage stress" is usually defined as when housing takes more than 30 per cent of after-tax income, but that definition varies with income. Obviously, if you're making $1 million a year after tax, being left with $700,000 for everything else is not very stressful at all. But if your wage is $50,000 and you're left with $582 a week after tax to look after a family, the stress of how to do that dominates your life.

The simplest way to examine the consequences of that upward shift in house prices is through the lens of The Average – that is, average earnings and median house prices. What's been the change in the percentage of income that a family on average wages has to devote to mortgage repayments? Well, it's basically impossible now for an average millennial family, earning the national average wage, with one adult working full-time and the other working three days a week, to buy a home for the national median price.

Here are the sums that lead to that conclusion:

> Wage one: $94,000 before tax, $71,100 after tax
> Wage two: $56,400 before tax, $46,500 after tax
> Total household income after tax: $117,600 per year
> Median Australian house price: $732,886
> A mortgage of 80 per cent of that (assuming a 20 per cent deposit): $527,073

Repayments at current variable mortgage rate of 6.9 per cent: $4117 per month

That's 42 per cent of household income – 12 per cent more than the measure of mortgage stress.

But with the 3 per cent buffer mandated by the regulator, APRA: $5297 per month.

That's $63,564 per year, or 54 per cent of household net income.

Loan declined.

In Sydney, where the median house price is now well over $1 million, it's much worse than the national average. That family would have to borrow $825,000 and repayments would be $5788 per month, 60 per cent of household income after tax, and leaving them $925.85 a week for food, petrol, utilities and clothes. That's if they could get a loan to buy a median house in the first place, which they couldn't, because the extra interest that banks have to notionally add to the mortgage rate now to ensure there's a buffer if rates go up is 3 per cent. So the interest rate that you're assessed on these days is 9.9 per cent, not 6.9 per cent, which gives a repayments-to-income ratio for our average family of 76 per cent. Declined, with a pitying smile.

Here's the same calculation in 2000, based on the national median house price at the time, for the same family with one adult working full-time and the other part-time, both on average weekly earnings, and using the tax scales in 2000.

Wage one: $43,352 before tax, $32,009 after tax

Wage two: $26,012 before tax, $24,206 after tax

Total household income after tax: $56,215 per year

Median Australian house price: $240,295

A mortgage of 80 per cent of that (assuming 20 per cent deposit): $192,236

Repayments at the prevailing mortgage rate of 8 per cent: $1494 per month

That's $17,928 a year, or 31.9 per cent of net family income —
tight but doable, and more importantly a bank would have
approved it. And note that interest rates were higher then.

Also, over the following ten years that family would have seen the value of
their house more than double, and their equity in it grow from a bit less than
$50,000 to about $350,000, a compound annual growth rate in their wealth
of more than 20 per cent. No wonder we've come to see housing as the best
way to create and grow wealth — because it's true! In ten years, that family
could upgrade to a bigger house for their growing brood, probably closer to
the city if they wanted.

In the real world, away from the averages and medians, it's worse. Let's
take as an example a nice three-bedroom, very ordinary weatherboard family
home at 35 Foch Street, Box Hill South, 20 kilometres from Melbourne's CBD.
This house sold recently for $1.65 million. To buy that place with a 20 per cent
deposit (assuming the buyer could come up with $330,000 cash) at current
interest rates and while keeping repayments below 30 per cent of household
income, a family would need to be bringing in $380,000 after tax, or more
than $600,000 a year in gross wages.

But no one on that sort of salary is buying a plain little house in Box Hill
South: they're looking 10 kilometres closer to the city in Malvern, with a
much larger deposit. The family buying 35 Foch Street would probably have
a deposit of a lot more than 20 per cent, either built up themselves or by tap-
ping the Bank of Mum and Dad (BMD).

By the way, that house sold eleven years ago, in 2012, for $614,000. At that
price, if a family was borrowing 80 per cent, given the interest rates and tax
scales at the time, they would have needed salaries before tax of $182,000 to
keep repayments to 30 per cent of net income. In 2012, that was 2.6 times
average weekly earnings; in 2023, the $640,000 salary needed to buy a $1.65
million house with a 20 per cent deposit is 6.8 times average weekly earnings.

So that's another, more real, way to express what has happened to housing in Australia. In ten years, the multiple of the average wage needed to buy
an ordinary little three-bedroom house in Box Hill South has almost tripled.

Another way to express this is: to get a three-bedroom family home now, if that couple who bought 35 Foch Street, Box Hill South in 2012 are still earning 2.6 times average weekly earnings, they would need to be looking another 10 kilometres away from the CBD, in Bayswater, Lalor or Tarneit. (The couple on *average* weekly earnings or below are renting; they're not buying anywhere.)

Sydney's much worse, of course. To get a three-bedroom family home there, you're looking in, say, Yagoona, 10 kilometres further out again and an hour on the train to the city. For a place that's the same distance from Sydney's CBD as Foch Street, Box Hill South is from Melbourne's CBD, you're up for a million dollars more.

One of the many reasons all this has happened is that the millennials' baby-boomer parents, who were in their late forties around 2000, started thinking about their retirement and investing in real estate, trying to supplement their super by negatively gearing a property and using the equity in their family home to do it.

What they didn't understand, or care about, was that by bidding up the price of houses with the negative gearing tax break, they were depriving their own children of the ability to buy a house and would have to make an early withdrawal from their own retirement funds to help them. Every family is different, of course, and most baby boomers with young kids wouldn't have joined the dots, but that's what happened.

One consequence of this now is the Bank of Mum and Dad – that is, baby boomers financing their millennial children into a house alongside the normal bank, or more likely mortgage broker, by bringing forward the transfer of some of their inheritance, usually to boost the deposit. And that makes some sense, because everybody is living longer so the inflated value of those boomer-owned houses won't get passed on — inheritance tax-free — to the next generation until it's far too late to be useful. The advent of the BMD is arguably just a sensible recognition of medical progress and the new longevity.

Eighteen months ago, the BMD became Australia's ninth-biggest home lender, with a loan book of $35 billion. But in addition to the loans is an unknown and unknowable number of gifts, which are likely to add up to much more than the repayable, interest-bearing loans that are known about. Apart from the prospect of Mum and Dad leaving themselves short in retirement in their eagerness to help the kids into a house, the problem is that not everybody has access to a BMD – not all mums and dads have that sort of money. Access to that bank for some is entrenching housing inequality.

And in any case, it only papers over the fundamental issue: that Australian homes have simply become too expensive for society to work normally. Early inheritance doesn't address the profound and complex changes that have been forced on Australian society by that one fact: that the price of a house has gone from three to four times income to seven to eight times income in the course of a generation.

It is not just Australia – something similar has happened in other countries as well, especially New Zealand and Canada. But this essay is about Australia, and every country's experience is unique. To be more specific, it's about before and after 2000, which is when things changed.

The most obvious thing, apart from the intergenerational inequality, is that home ownership has declined steadily for decades, despite much lower interest rates and unprecedented spending on first home buyer grants. What's more, the largest decline is for millennials and generation Z.

The decline in home ownership has many consequences, both economic and social, including a lack of security. One thing that's been getting a lot of attention has been a shortage of rental properties: less ownership means more renting, but construction has simply not been keeping up with demand, especially with the boom in immigration this year, since migrants mostly rent at first. This has exacerbated a rental property shortage that has been bubbling since immigration doubled in 2006.

The national capital-city rental vacancy rate is now down to a record low of 1 per cent, compared to a ten-year average of 2.8 per cent, with the result that rents are rising well above the inflation rate. Apart from the financial stress this is causing many families, it's also resulting in an increase in homelessness and rough living as well as in average household size, since more people are forced to move in together.

The rental crisis is largely the result of declining home ownership, because fewer people can afford to buy a place but in many suburbs rents have risen so much that it's becoming more expensive to rent. And this is happening despite the tax breaks that property investors get from negative gearing and the capital gains tax discount, which are meant to boost the supply of rental accommodation. They obviously don't.

In fact, those tax deductions for individual investors tend to work against rental supply because they keep out institutional investors who might built apartment blocks to hold and rent out. The property development business model favours selling apartments to individual investors who can pay more than big super funds because they get tax breaks that super funds don't. The government is talking about using tax breaks to encourage built-to-rent by institutions, but these would just offset the tax breaks that individuals get – so

Figure 4 Home ownership rate (%) by age group, 1971–2021

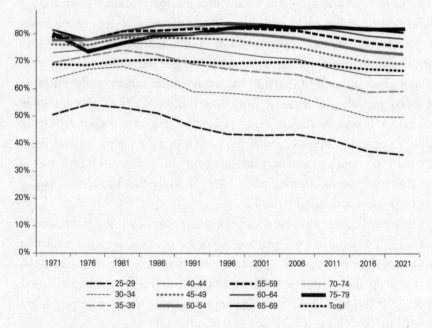

Source: AIHW analysis of customised ABS Census data, 2022.

it will be a case of competing tax breaks. Perhaps it would be better to just get rid of the tax breaks altogether and let the market work it out.

One consequence of the decline in house prices that is rarely mentioned but I think may be psychologically important is pet ownership. As home ownership declines, so does the ability to have a pet. Another way to look at it is that the difficulty of having a dog or cat in a rental property is a big part of the reason Australians prefer to own a place rather than rent.

Ten years ago my wife and I decided to renovate our house and had to move out for more than twelve months. We had two Labradors and a ginger cat, and tried to rent a place for the duration of the renovation – no dice. Our animals were banned wherever we tried, so we borrowed to the hilt (on top of the renovation) and bought an investment property instead, and we lived in that much smaller place while the renovation took longer than expected. It turned out

Figure 5 Rental vacancy rate, 2013–2023

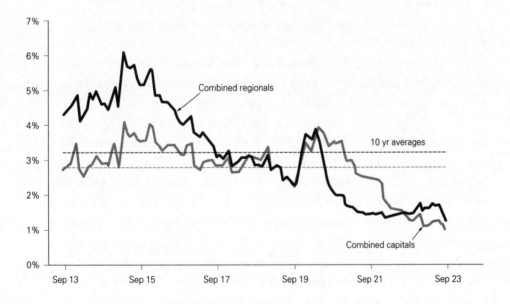

Source: CoreLogic.

to be the best investment we ever made, and entrenched our view that debt-funded housing is the best way to create wealth, but we wouldn't have done it if we'd been allowed to have our beloved dogs and cat in a rental property.

Tenant laws have been changing lately, and in two Australian states landlords aren't allowed to automatically ban pets. In both Victoria and Queensland, tenants can fill out a pet request form. In Victoria, landlords have to provide a good reason to disallow them, while in Queensland there's a list of reasons for landlords to say no, including that the property is too small or the pets might be dangerous, so it is pretty easy for pets to be denied. In every other state or territory, it's still just up the landlord. Despite that, Victoria has by far the smallest proportion of rental properties that allow pets.

Across Australia in September 2023 there were 55,078 houses and flats advertised for rent on realestate.com.au, of which 7905 were still available to rent after I ticked the box marked "pets considered." That's just 14.4 per cent of all rental properties in Australia for which pets will be "considered." In Victoria, where pets are supposedly allowed, it's half that: 7 per cent.

There's already a rental crisis across the country, with hopeful tenants lining up at open-for-inspections and suffering endless heartbreaking rejections, but if you've got a cat or, god forbid, a large dog, forget it – you have to buy a place or get rid of the animal. Even in Queensland, the most lenient state in the country, less than a quarter of the places are available to you.

Earlier this year, a national survey found that 61 per cent of Australian households own pets, and 90 per cent have owned a pet at some stage. But only 36 per cent of those pet owners are renters, according to the survey. Meanwhile, study after study reveals that there are many health benefits of owning a pet. But to a large extent the only way to do so is to own a house, and not rent. Millennials and generation Z were often brought up with pets around them but now find that the difficulty of affording a house as adults means they can't bring up their own children with pets in the same way.

The high cost of home ownership is socially corrosive in other ways. Young families saving for a deposit often have to live with parents and/or in-laws for much longer than they, or the parents, would like, and it is probably contributing to the decline in the fertility rate from 3.4 births per woman in 1958 to 1.5 now, not to mention the sheer tension of living with in-laws and the decline in living standards from being crammed in.

Young families, when they eventually buy a place, are usually forced to live much further from the city than they did with their parents, and not only spend hours commuting but also live with fewer amenities around them and live a long way from their parents, and the grandparents of their children.

And then there's the more straightforward problem that devoting a larger share of income to mortgage repayments means less disposable income for things such as travel and eating out. Repayments as a proportion of income had been falling in recent years because of declining interest rates. But some families are extremely vulnerable to the normalisation of interest rates in the past eighteen months. The cost-of-living crisis that has dominated both politics and economics in 2023 is all about young families with big mortgages doing it tough.

There are broader economic problems caused by expensive houses, as well as the individual ones for families affected by it. As the Committee for Economic Development in Australia (CEDA) wrote in a paper in 2017, "when housing affordability becomes a national issue, economic growth is undermined in a number of ways." Being forced to live a long way out of the city, with long commutes, reduces productivity, as does traffic congestion and long delivery times.

High levels of debt make the economy and financial system more fragile. The Reserve Bank estimated earlier this year that 15 per cent of households will be in negative cashflow by the end of 2023, so many are in it now. But market research firm Roy Morgan upped the ante with a survey early this year that suggested 1.1 million mortgage holders, or 23.9 per cent of all mortgage owners, are "at risk" of mortgage stress as a result of the so-called mortgage cliff, where borrowers come off cheap fixed-rate loans onto more expensive variable-rate ones.

"Mortgage stress" dropped to record lows during 2021 because low interest rates, government support and the measures taken by banks to support

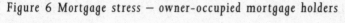

Figure 6 Mortgage stress — owner-occupied mortgage holders

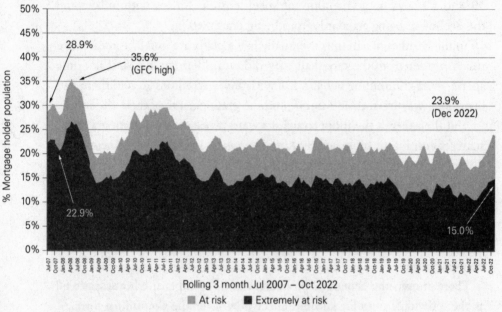

Source: Roy Morgan.

borrowers in financial distress all combined to reduce the number of mortgage holders considered "at risk." But the number of mortgage holders considered "extremely at risk" increased to 666,000 (15 per cent) in the three months to December 2022, which is in line with the long-term average.

And debt begets debt. There's been a big increase in the number of credit card accounts being opened, which suggests people are turning to debt to get through the cost-of-living crunch caused by the combination of rising prices and rising interest rates (decreed by the RBA to combat the rising prices). Credit reporting agency Equifax says there's been a 31 per cent increase in new cards opened this year, with a particularly big rise among first home buyers who had previously closed their card accounts to boost their mortgage borrowing capacity.

Now let's turn to the origins of Australia's housing problem, and in particular the problem of supply.

HOW IT STARTED

Australia's first land sale happened on 14 January 1826, to John Macarthur, a few years before he was declared insane, clapped in a straitjacket and died. Macarthur, whose picture adorned our two-dollar banknote between 1966 and 1988, was already very wealthy, first from peddling rum, as one of the many criminals in the New South Wales Rum Corps of racketeering soldiers, and then as a prosperous and influential landowner and pastoralist. That came after his mate Lieutenant Governor Francis Grose granted him 200 acres of prime grazing land near Parramatta. Grose was only in charge for two years, but it was long enough for him to set up the Macarthurs. John Macarthur called it Elizabeth Farm, after his wife, and the house they built is still there, at 70 Alice Street, Rosehill.

Macarthur's grant of land was typical – most of the real estate transactions in those days were free grants to settlers and ex-convicts, although there were some sales, typically at £1 per acre. Settlers could also acquire land by simply occupying it and using it for a period of time without the permission of the government. This was a common practice in the early days of settlement, when the government did not have the resources to keep track of what was going on.

Of course, the very existence of a real estate market in those days, and in particular the appalling idea of free land grants to British settlers and ex-convicts, relied on the idea that Australia was terra nullius – that is, no one owned it before the British. That legal fiction came from Captain James Cook claiming it for the English Crown on 22 August 1770. His instructions from King George III contained this passage: "You are also with the Consent of the Natives to take possession of Convenient Situations in the Country in the Name of the King of Great Britain: Or: if you find the Country uninhabited take Possession for his Majesty by setting up proper Marks & Inscriptions, as first discoverers and possessors."

Needless to say, Cook took possession, but not with consent. In an essay written in 1968, the anthropologist W.E.H. Stanner wrote: "It is a matter of history that he did not obey the instructions. He did not find the country uninhabited and it is certainly not with the consent of the natives that he took possession of a part of New Holland."

Governor Arthur Phillip and all his successors acted as if the second part of Cook's instructions applied, that New Holland was "waste and unoccupied." They were applying the Doctrine of Discovery, which dated back to the mid-fifteenth century, when Pope Nicholas V authorised King Afonso of Portugal to subjugate "all Saracens and pagans whatsover, and other enemies of Christ wheresoever placed," and "reduce their persons to perpetual servitude," to take their belongings, including land, "to convert them to his, and [his successors'] use." That papal bull became the basis of all colonialism, as well as the slavery that underpinned British and European wealth for the next 500 years.

The Doctrine of Discovery was even upheld in the US Supreme Court in 1823 as a generally accepted principle of international law. Under that law England was able to say that it owned all of Australia, and, having established some of it as a prison, could start giving bits of the place – completely ignoring the original owners – to whomever the governor of the time felt happy with.

There was one significant land transaction in which real estate was actually bought from the Aborigines, although historians are pretty clear that the sellers didn't understand what was going on, as the very notion of owning land was alien to them. It happened on 6 June 1835, when John Batman, who was coincidentally born at Rosehill in 1801 and was not a very nice man at all, having murdered dozens of First Australians in Tasmania, agreed to pay the Wurundjeri people of the Kulin nation a yearly rent of forty pairs of blankets, forty-two tomahawks, 130 knives, sixty-two pairs of scissors, forty looking glasses, 250 handkerchiefs, eighteen shirts, four flannel jackets, four suits of clothes and 150 lb of flour, for 600,000 acres on the banks of the Yarra River.

Say what you like about John Batman, at least he was acknowledging that the land was owned by someone other than the King of England, and wasn't terra nullius. He called it "Batmania," so it's a good thing the scheme didn't last, since these days it would be confused with a superhero film, and he famously declared that "this will be the place for a village." He was just getting ready to build his eponymous town on the banks of the Yarra, the land that he had bought fair and square from its owners, when on 26 August 1835 Governor Richard Bourke in Sydney issued a proclamation declaring the transaction was "void and of no effect as [it is] against the rights of the Crown."

The Secretary of State for the Colonies, Lord Glenelg, acceded to Bourke's cancellation of Batman's deal with the Wurundjeri people, saying that he would not recognise in the Aborigines "any right to alienate to private adventurers the land of the colony ... such a concession would subvert the foundation of on which all proprietary rights in New South Wales at present rest."

So the Crown compulsorily acquired the land back from Batman and the place was named after the prime minister of England, Viscount Melbourne. Governor Bourke was immortalised by the main road up the middle of the city being named after him.

I'm retelling these stories here because the land rush that resulted from the dishing out of land for free to those favoured by usually corrupt governors, along with the squelching of the only actual transaction in which land was bought from the original owners, is one of the two rushes at the heart of a paradox in Australians' attitude to land. The other is the gold rush of the 1850s, which led to the great land boom of the 1880s, in turn born from its scarcity.

The paradox is that Australians regard land as both abundant and scarce enough for speculation. That attitude has been explosive for house prices because urban construction spread far and wide and land in cities was squandered rather than carefully preserved with medium-density building. At the same time, the nineteenth-century land boom after the gold rush kicked off the idea that land speculation is the basis for wealth creation. After World War II, fifty years after the first boom, that part of our culture was rediscovered, but land close to the cities was found to be in short supply – large blocks with one house on them stretched into the distance. Despite the abundance of land in this vast island continent, it really was scarce enough for speculation to flourish.

The scarcity had its beginnings in 1851, when gold was discovered at Clunes in Victoria and Orange in New South Wales. By 1890, Australia's population had ballooned from 400,000 to 3.2 million. More relevant to the nation's first real estate bubble was a baby boom that got underway in 1860: those babies became adults between 1880 and 1890 and started looking for a place of their own. The growth in Australia's adult population averaged about 2.5 per cent a year in the 1860s and 1870s, but then accelerated to 4 per cent a year in the 1880s.

The Victorian gold rush proved to be more frenzied, and more lucrative, than the one in New South Wales, and led to a wild property bubble in Melbourne in the 1880s, financed entirely by bank lending. There was almost as much of a boom in the number of banks as in land prices, and in 1887 *The Argus* carried a story about what it called the "Earth Hunger": "Earth hunger has always distinguished the Anglo-Saxon race. And a piece of land, if judiciously bought, is acknowledged to be one of his safest investments."

By 1888, all the easy gold had been found and prospectors drifted away. Population began to decline and after a boom in construction there was a housing surplus. The market peaked in 1889 and prices began to collapse, and Melbourne became the epicentre of a very big bust, and then depression. Nigel Stapledon of the School of Economics at UNSW says that Melbourne prices rose about 64 per cent in real terms from 1880 to their peak in 1889, then fell by 51 per cent to a trough in the mid-1890s. He goes on: "To put that 1889 peak in perspective, prices in Melbourne did not revisit their 1889 levels until over sixty years later in 1950."

As for Sydney, Stapledon says:

> The 1880s–90s price cycle in Sydney, in keeping with its less dramatic cycle in population growth, was less extreme than Melbourne's experience but still stands out. Sydney median prices rose 32 per cent

in the 1880s to a peak in 1892; that is, there was a lag of a few years after Melbourne prices peaked and started their sharp decline. The subsequent fall was about 36 per cent so that, while the boom had been less pronounced than Melbourne's experience, the immediate pain was still significant.

By 1890 banks started to get into trouble, and this was exacerbated by the Barings crisis in London, in which that bank had to be bailed out after getting caught with bad loans in Argentina, which had had a similar property bubble and bust to the one Australia was heading into. The Bank of Van Diemen's Land was the first to go, in 1891, and thirteen others soon followed. The colonies of New South Wales and Victoria suffered their first, and still most severe, economic depression – worse than the Great Depression of the 1930s.

During 1892 and 1893, GDP fell 17 per cent, and fifty-four of the sixty-four institutions that called themselves banks (a lot of them were building societies) operating in 1891 had closed by mid-1893, thirty-four of them permanently. At the height of the crisis in April and May 1893, the banks that had shut their doors and suspended payment accounted for 56 per cent of deposits and 61 per cent of the notes issued in the six Australian colonies.

But while the aftermath of the boom of the 1880s was horrible, and took a long time to get over, the idea of real estate as an investment asset had been established, albeit "judiciously bought," as The Argus put it, which was not always the case, and still isn't. And the idea that land was plentiful and easily attained had been established in the first few decades of the colony and led to the sprawl of Australian cities and the dream that everyone (except the original inhabitants, of course) could acquire a quarter of an acre on which to build their family castle. That dream has turned into a nightmare of blocks that are one-tenth of an acre, on which are squeezed houses that are enormous: no room for a Hills Hoist anymore.

So the treatment of land in Australia's first century created the conditions and attitudes that led to the housing crisis of its third century. First, the problem of not enough medium-density housing close to the city – because, well, who needs it when everyone can have a quarter of an acre? – has led to a crisis of supply. And second is the treatment of housing as not just somewhere to live but also the greatest of investment assets with which to build wealth.

Australia had two rushes that swelled the population and set us up for a dysfunctional attitude towards land: the rush for land itself after 1788, and the second one, for gold, after 1851.

As discussed above, state and local governments have the job of restricting the supply of housing, but before dealing with that in more detail, there are two other things to look at first. There is one supply job at which the federal government started well and then failed: public housing. The other thing is the way we have all crowded into a few cities that each have one CBD, and then sprawled.

SUPPLY PROBLEM 1: PUBLIC HOUSING

The first four decades of the twentieth century were largely characterised by an oversupply of housing, a hangover from World War I. This was caused by the halt to immigration during the war and the absence of so many soldiers. Constant oversupply meant prices were relatively stable.

Prices fell in the Great Depression, but not as much as in the 1890s because the boom in the 1920s wasn't as great as the bubble in the 1880s. What did happen in the 1930s depression, though, was a collapse in home building, so that new supply fell below population growth and the oversupply from World War I was absorbed. There was also a huge increase in the slums that had always existed to some extent in the cities.

In 1939, when war broke out again, the government used wartime powers to fix rents across the country, copying both the United Kingdom and the United States. Then, in 1942, Prime Minister John Curtin did something that neither the US nor the UK did: he extended price controls to house and land purchases as well. It was part of a National Economic Plan that included pegging wages and profits and closing non-essential industries. And in May 1942, Curtin took over the power to levy income tax from the states, which was a turning point for the national economy, and for both the constitution and federal–state relations.

House prices were set at no more than 10 per cent above "fair value," as determined by an approved valuer. As you can imagine, there was a lot of pressure on valuers to come up with higher fair values, especially as inflation started to take off, and owners also tried to get around the law by jacking up the price of furniture that went with the houses. When that loophole was closed, they started requiring "key money," which proved harder to stop.

Those laws lapsed in 1946, but the government – now led by Ben Chifley – wanted to keep control of house prices and rents, and used the *Defence (Transitional Provisions) Act* to do it. Then, in May 1948, Chifley held a referendum to give the government permanent control of house prices and rents in the constitution. It was a spectacular failure. He wanted to insert into section 51 of the constitution a clause that gave parliament the power to make laws with respect to "rents and prices (including charges)." It lost 59.34 per cent to 40.66 per cent, with 99 per cent of the population voting – a comprehensive rejection.

But Chifley's argument in favour of the proposal still resonates today and bears repeating. He said it was needed "because rising prices threaten the value of wages or salaries, and of savings, and undermine the stability of the economy." It may have been the second part of his argument that lost him the vote. He also said: "the Government can be relied on to administer price control sanely, to decentralise as much as possible, and to remove controls as supplies become adequate." Sanely? And remove controls later? Yeah right, said Australia.

By the way, Gough Whitlam had another go at it in December 1973, a year after becoming prime minister, with a referendum that would have given the government the power to control all prices, including house prices. That was defeated like the one in 1948, although Whitlam managed to increase the Yes vote to 43.81 per cent – still nowhere near enough.

Back to 1950. When controls were eventually lifted, house prices more than doubled. In Sydney, the median price surged 119 per cent, putting it 53 per cent above the 1942 level in real terms, a third more than the increase in building costs from 1942 to 1950. After controls were lifted, there were also dire shortages of building materials and labour, so construction costs rose rapidly as well. In Melbourne, the rise in real terms was 79 per cent above the 1942 level.

The biggest problems with housing after World War II were the shortages caused by the wartime price and rent controls, and the terrible slums in every city left over from the Great Depression of the 1930s. A Housing Investigation and Slum Abolition Board was established in 1935 to investigate the extent of slum housing and to recommend solutions. The board published its report in 1937, finding that there were more than 100,000 such dwellings in Australia, housing at least 500,000 people.

It wrote: "The Board records its horror and amazement at the deplorable conditions ... Hidden behind wide, spacious streets there are slum pockets which are hotbeds of depravity and disease." We're talking dwellings that barely qualified as houses at all – no bathrooms or sewerage, leaky roofs and holes in the walls. Hotbeds, mainly, of human misery.

The board recommended slum clearances and a lot of new construction, which led, momentously, to the Commonwealth Housing Commission (CHC) being set up in 1938 and to housing laws in most states. Progress on public housing was then derailed by the war, and it wasn't until 1945 that a Commonwealth State Housing Agreement (CSHA) was created to provide federal funds to the states for the purpose, supported and directed by the CHC.

The CSHA was the beginning of the first and only serious national housing policy in Australia, and when the last such agreement ended in 2003 that was the end of housing policies. The original CSHA laid out a series of ambitious objectives and how they could be funded, and it was underpinned by a groundbreaking report in 1944 by the CHC that recognised, for the first time, that government had a responsibility for ensuring that all citizens have affordable access to a house.

The chairman of the CHC at the time had been a fine batsman for Queensland with the equally fine name of Leo Patrick Devereaux O'Connor, who seems to have finished his cricket career with a very solid batting average. But his work on Australian housing was even better.

The report that he wrote with his four fellow commissioners led off with these ringing words:

> We consider that a dwelling of good standard and equipment is not only the need, but the right of every citizen – whether the dwelling is to be rented or purchased, no tenant or purchaser should be exploited by excessive profit.
>
> The overwhelming impression obtained from our inquiries is one of widespread deficiencies in the quantity and quality of pre-war housing and the acuteness of the present shortage. We feel

strongly that action should be taken immediately to alleviate this shortage ... action should be taken immediately to acquire land, prepare sites by surveys and provision of services, and prepare plans and working drawings for post-war homes, so that building may be increased rapidly as soon as further supplies of labour and materials are available.

They even laid out in detail the recommended specifications of a "government-sponsored house" – that is, houses built by the government and rented cheaply to the poor – including the size of each room, the height of the ceilings (nine feet) and interior finishes. The kitchen fittings "should be arranged in logical sequence in regard to their functions so as to minimise movements by the housewife." And the allotment size should be not less than 4500 square feet. That's about one-tenth of an acre, by the way.

Those details, and the sequence of the kitchen fittings, might be explained by the fact that the report was drafted by the CHC's secretary, Mary Willmott Phillips (whose husband, J.G. Phillips, went on to become governor of the Reserve Bank of Australia). Another woman, Mary Ryan, was a member of the five-person commission. She was an ALP branch president and leader of the Country Women's Association. The *Australian Dictionary of Biography* notes that "Mrs Ryan's warm personality, generosity and sense of humour made her a popular and respected figure; J.B. Chifley was among the regular visitors to her home ... Her own experience in a house with no electricity (save for lighting), no internal water and only a coal-fired stove proved invaluable to the commission in detailing the conditions in which many housewives worked."

These two women were enormously important in the shaping of Australia's early housing policy. In his book *Accommodating Australians: Commonwealth involvement in housing*, Professor Patrick Troy says: "Ryan and Willmott Phillips' contributions to the CHC's deliberations ensured that the community's views on housing issues were sought and that the emerging concerns of women on housing were broadly discussed in papers and magazines and were given proper weight."

The CHC estimated that there was a shortage of 300,000 houses in 1945, adding that the number could be "far greater" than that. The first CSHA that came out of Leo O'Connor's report was signed that same year. It got off to a rocky start: Queensland refused to sign because it didn't allow the houses to be sold, South Australia thought its own scheme was better and stayed out, and Tasmania joined and then pulled out because of the rule against sales. More importantly, the number of houses that resulted didn't make much of a dent on the shortage, because money, labour and materials were all in short supply after the war. In the first year of CSHA funding, state housing authorities built just over 4000 houses, which was 26 per cent of all houses built nationally, and that fell to 14.8 per cent in the second year.

When Robert Menzies became prime minister for the second time in December 1949, the controls on house prices and rents had just been lifted. The key issue in the election was bank nationalisation: Menzies campaigned successfully that he would repeal Ben Chifley's *Bank Nationalisation Act* of 1945. But Menzies was much more interested in housing than banking, because he believed that home ownership would create "little capitalists" who would vote Liberal. In his 1949 campaign speech, he devoted a section to it which is worth quoting in full:

> Except in relation to the Territories and War Service Homes, the direct responsibility for housing is with the State Governments. But the Commonwealth must accept large obligations of assistance. There is already a Commonwealth-States Housing Agreement. We will seek its amendment so as to permit and aid "little Capitalists" to own their own homes.
>
> We will attack the basic causes of under-production and excessive cost. While shortages continue, we will facilitate the entry of selected imported building materials; and will also review the incidence of such imposts as Sales Tax on home fittings and furniture.
>
> The limitation of output which is so notorious a factor in the present almost impossible cost of a home is partly due to a view in the building trades that past slumps in building activity will occur

again, and that it will therefore pay not to get through the building programme too quickly. This policy produces great hardship for hundreds of thousands of wage-earners who cannot afford the present prices. The answer to it is that the demand for building should be as far as possible stabilised. This can be done if Governments, Departments, and Housing Commissions plan their slum clearance and reconstruction works for periods when private building falls off. In the desire to guarantee a continuation of steady annual demand in this vital industry, this will be our policy if elected.

By 1950 the number of dwellings built by the CHC annually had increased to 56,987, and the scheme was ticking along nicely. There was still a big backlog, though, and the states were also failing to build enough infrastructure, mainly water and sewerage. That was partly because the Commonwealth had taken off them the ability to levy income taxes, so they were short of money; thus began the great "fiscal imbalance," as it's still called.

Nevertheless, between 1945 and 1955, 96,000 homes for rent were built by state governments, funded by the Commonwealth – 14.4 per cent of all houses that were built nationally. But then Sir William "Bill" Spooner, a tough former soldier at Gallipoli who became Menzies' Minister for Social Services with responsibility for housing, began undermining the CSHA, arguing that it was not "fair" to sell to low-income workers on favourable terms because they "had no culture of thrift or sense of community obligation," which was pretty rough from a so-called minister for social services. He was basically saying it was unfair to the middle classes, echoing Menzies' exalting of the "forgotten people" in his famous 1942 radio speech. They later became John Howard's "battlers."

Menzies claimed that he and Bill Spooner built more public housing than Chifley did, which was probably true because they were at it for longer. But in 1954 Spooner changed the rules to allow the houses to be bought on favourable terms by middle-class people who weren't living in them, instead of allowing them to be sold only to the tenants (also on favourable terms). Bob Menzies gets a lot of credit for expanding access to housing, and in particular for spending money on public housing, but it's unjustified in my view. He and Spooner destroyed it and set the scene for decades of mistakes by their successors in the Coalition.

Between 1947 and 1961, the housing stock in Australia increased by 50 per cent, about 10 per cent more than the increase in population. Economist Saul Eslake says that governments directly built 221,700, or 24 per cent of the total increase, through programs financed under the Commonwealth–State Housing Agreements, or under the War and Defence Service Homes loan scheme, or both. And during this period, the rate of home ownership surged from 53.4 per cent to 71.4 per cent in 1966 – the largest increase in home ownership in Australia's history.

*

There was another, darker side to what Menzies was doing, which added to the legacies of the land rush and gold rush of the nineteenth century to bring a third negative element to Australia's housing culture and the way Australians think about it. The quote from him earlier, that "one of the best instincts in us is that which induces us to have one little piece of earth with a house and a garden which is ours," was taken into Australians' souls as a kind of moral imperative.

The late Professor Troy of ANU, one of the nation's greatest urban planners, wrote in a paper on public housing that "home owners were seen as 'men of substance,' pillars of the community, while renters were seen as feckless transients with no connection with the community and no desire to be engaged." Bob Menzies and Bill Spooner hated renters because they believed them to be politically biased and more likely to vote Labor. Spooner even commissioned research by the Liberal Party's secretariat to determine the extent of the bias (its findings turned out to be inconclusive).

But by the time Spooner and Menzies retired, in 1965 and 1966 respectively, two things had happened: the ideal of home ownership had been elevated to an almost religious status in Australia, and the destruction of public housing was well underway. Menzies always took credit for the rate of home ownership increasing from close to 50 per cent to more than 70 per cent – and it probably did help keep him in power for seventeen years – but he had already planted the seeds of its decline, and home ownership started falling as soon as he quit. It is now around 66 per cent.

And in any case, none of those home ownership numbers is all that impressive on a global scale. At 66.3 per cent, Australia sits fifty-third on the world home ownership league table, below Europe's 69.9 per cent and just above the United States' 65.9 per cent. There are nine countries above 90 per cent, according to Wikipedia, and China is just under that at 89.68 per cent. Australia's home ownership rate is pretty much average: no big deal.

In a way, Menzies can take some credit for the big increase in home ownership up to 1966 because it was largely due to the aggressive selling of public housing stock by the states, which he and Spooner forced on them to create a class of capitalists who would vote Liberal. The other cause – nothing to do with Menzies – was the massive uptake of war service loans by returned servicepeople like my father. According to the Australian War Memorial, by 1966, when Menzies retired, 102,200 war service loans had been made in Australia for a total value of $1.2 billion. Of these, 94,300 were made to veterans of World War II.

During the 1950s and '60s under Menzies, public housing increasingly became a matter of welfare and social services rather than supporting the "right of every citizen" that Leo O'Connor wrote about in 1945. When Ben Chifley was PM, there was a minister for works and housing; after Menzies took over in 1949, housing came under the minister for social services, where it has stayed ever since. It doesn't belong there: housing is not welfare, it's an economic right.

Professor Troy notes that by 1971 approximately 40 per cent of the houses built under the CSHA had been sold to Menzies' "little capitalists," squeezing out those who actually needed social housing. "One consequence of this was that State authorities developed housing on the fringe of the cities. Low income households were increasingly forced into outer locations where job opportunities were few and transport costs high." Also, the number of public dwellings built as high-rise apartments grew steadily, and the number as houses declined. Says Troy: "The process of changing the form of Australian cities was speeding up as was the proportion of publicly owned dwellings as flats."

Despite all this, in his submission to the Senate Economics Committee in 2013, Saul Eslake said that from 1947 to 1976 federal and state government housing policies were principally directed towards increasing the supply of housing, and at increasing or maintaining home ownership rates, even if under Menzies they had the overriding purpose of entrenching the Liberal Party in power. And these policies actually achieved all those objectives.

The election of Malcolm Fraser at the end of 1975 brought that to an end. By 1978 the idea that public housing was a right for all had been fully dismantled. It had become nothing more than a form of welfare for the neediest. This profound shift was both ideological and driven by cost-cutting. In the 1978 CHSA, Fraser insisted that the states charge market rents and provide rebates for the neediest; he was trying to save money but was also philosophically opposed to public housing.

Near the end of Fraser's eight years in office, in 1982, public housing completions under the CSHA had fallen to 7101, the lowest number since 1948, and Bob Hawke swept into office promising to turn this around, but with a twist. The ALP's housing policy, released in November 1982, had said:

> Labor will lift homebuilding activity to 135,000 starts in its first year, 145,000 in the second year and 160,000 in third and subsequent years ... Labor is opposed to deregulation of the financial system ... An ALP government will set up a Department of Housing and Urban and Regional Affairs ... An ALP government will expand and upgrade the supply of public housing, with a goal of doubling over 10 years the proportion of total dwelling stock held in a variety of public tenures through state and local initiatives.

After he knocked off Bill Hayden as ALP leader on 8 February 1983, Hawke changed that policy to emphasise private construction and ownership. The earlier promise to double public housing was dropped.

The housing industry was a prominent part of Hawke's National Economic Summit in April 1983, and housing starts surged from 105,000 in Fraser's last year to 153,000 in 1984. Hawke then made a big deal of housing in his 1984 campaign speech:

> We pledged ourselves to bring homeownership once again within the reach of ordinary Australian families – and to end the sense of despair and frustration that was beginning to engulf thousands upon thousands of young people seeking their own homes. We have increased public housing support by fifty per cent. We introduced the First Home Owners Scheme, to bring home ownership within the reach of thousands of young Australians of limited means. The number of new houses being built in Australia has increased by one third. And we are going to keep it that way. In the next twelve months, 145,000 new houses will be built in Australia, an increase of forty per cent over the level of two years ago. And beyond the next year we will maintain at least this level of housing activity, and ensure that our housing industry never again slumps into the contraction and despair of the year before we were called into office.

Note that his 1983 "promise" of 160,000 had been quietly cut to 145,000, while still being presented as an ambitious target. Housing completions started falling immediately after the 1984 election and didn't hit Hawke's target until 1989. Promises like that about housing, followed by a total failure to meet them, became a staple of campaign politics thereafter, emphasising the importance of at least appearing to care about housing while not actually doing much.

Most prime ministers, especially Labor ones, seeking election or re-election promise to build houses, the latest being Anthony Albanese with his plan for 1.2 million houses over five years.

Albanese's foray into housing began in October 2022 with a "National Housing Accord" agreed with the states that would result in 1 million new houses over five years. That was accurately described in the document as an "aspirational target," which means that it was not a promise and was not supported by any actual policies.

At that point, the most recent housing completions data from the ABS was for the June quarter, during which 43,649 dwellings were built. If that rate continued for five years, then 872,980 dwellings would be built, so the aspiration of 1 million over five years would be an increase of 14.6 per cent. In fact, in the five years before the pandemic, 1,028,480 dwellings were built, so they were really just aspiring to get the amount of house building back to what it was pre-COVID.

Awkwardly, completions promptly fell to 38,710 in the quarter following the announcement of the aspirational target. Then at another National Cabinet meeting in August 2023, the ante was upped by 20 per cent to 1.2 million houses over five years. The extra 200,000 houses (which means a total of 240,000 per year, or 657 new houses per day) are to be achieved with a bounty of $15,000 per house paid to state governments for releasing land, capped at $3 billion – so 200,000 bounties.

In October 2022, when they came up with the original 1 million aspiration, the states all agreed, among other things, to "undertake expedited zoning, planning and land release to deliver the joint commitment on social and affordable housing in well located areas, including looking for immediate opportunities to free up well located state land, for example in and around train stations and TAFE campuses including for affordable housing."

So apparently $15,000 per house will entice them to do 20 per cent more than they had already promised, which was a pretty full and politically dangerous promise to begin with – freeing up land in "well-located" areas tends to annoy a lot of existing residents, otherwise known as NIMBYs ("not in my backyard"). The Albanese policy seems to be based on the idea that state and local governments are so desperate for cash they'll do anything for $15,000 – even destroy their own re-election chances by annoying the NIMBYs who elected them with apartment towers sprinkled through the leafy suburbs.

In any case, state governments and local councils don't build houses and apartments – developers do. Even if 1.2 million lots are released over five years, developers will only build on them if they can make a profit, which applies to all political promises about housing.

As far as I can tell, the total number of houses "promised" during election campaigns by aspiring prime ministers between 1955 and 2022 is close to 9 million.

According to the Australian Bureau of Statistics, the total number of dwellings actually built in Australia since 1955 is 6.7 million.

Shortfall: 2.3 million

Those houses would be handy now.

The decline in public housing after the mid-1960s is far from the only reason for the crushing shortfall in Australian housing over the past seventy years; it isn't even the main one, although the disappearance of public housing has removed what had been a steady flow of affordable housing. The main thing is the shape of Australian cities and the way planning works.

When Australia became a Federation on 1 January 1901, the population was 3,788,123 according to the census taken that year. One million people, or 26 per cent, lived in Melbourne and Sydney, and there were few people in the other capital cities. In the mid-1930s, when both Melbourne and Sydney each passed 1 million residents within a few years of each other, the Australian population had grown to 6.9 million, so the proportion in the main capital cities was still under 30 per cent.

Now 67 per cent of Australia's population live in a capital city and 40 per cent are in Melbourne and Sydney, more than the proportion that lived in all capital cities less than a century ago. If you include all cities, not just capitals, 91.9 per cent of Australians are urbanites, so less than a tenth live in the bush. According to data produced by the World Resources Institute, that puts Australia about fifth in the world in crowding into cities, if you exclude countries that are basically just a city, such as Bermuda, Monaco and Hong Kong. That 91.9 per cent today compares with 77 per cent in 1950 and with a global average of 62.8 per cent – which has itself doubled since 1950, so the trend around the world is also towards greater urbanisation. But with three people per square kilometre, Australia also has the distinction of being the fifth most sparsely population country on earth, after Greenland, Western Sahara, Mongolia and Namibia.

Why did sparse Australia become so urbanised? Obviously, the main reason is that 18 per cent of the country is covered by ten deserts, and a lot of the rest is very dry as well. But there are plenty of cities in deserts around the world. Another reason is that the distances are enormous, so if you don't live in a city you have a long trip to get to a doctor or a decent supermarket. On the positive side, there are the things that act as magnets, common to all cities: jobs, education, healthcare, culture, shopping and restaurants.

While a push to decentralise has been part of the national political narrative for more than a century, various efforts at achieving it over the years have never worked. Most of it was political lip service, though there have been a few genuine attempts to get Australians to move to the bush.

Not long after Federation there was a series of "land settlement schemes" aimed explicitly at decentralisation in which the government sold acreage to would-be farmers on favourable time-payment terms, with loans for the tractors and fences as well. They were even trained in farming and driving tractors, and given after-sales service.

But it didn't work because most of the settlers from the city were hopeless farmers, and the land they were plonked on was poor quality. Those who lasted on their farms until 1930 gave up when the Depression hit.

The soldier settlement schemes after World War I were a little more successful, perhaps because the men who had returned from the trenches were hard workers, but in the end this didn't work either. Most of them were city boys at heart, and gravitated back to the big smoke.

The 1964 Premiers' Conference set up the Commonwealth/State Officials' Committee on Decentralisation, comprising a football team of bureaucrats. They rushed out their final report six years later, in July 1972, five months before the Labor Party, led by Whitlam, won its first election since 1946, when Chifley beat Menzies first time around.

In 1973, Whitlam became an enthusiastic convert to decentralisation and for the first time discussion began to focus on the relocation of manufacturing and service activities into non-metropolitan areas, rather than just extending agriculture. In a submission to the Productivity Commission some years later, regional development researcher Paul Collits wrote: "The most radical move was the creation of the legendary Department of Urban and Regional Development (DURD) and the Cities Commission. These bodies, especially DURD, were to set the scene for a dramatic shake up of bureaucratic politics in Canberra, greatly resisted by Treasury, that would introduce a focus on spatial issues at the heart of government."

Whitlam and his minister for community development and regional affairs, Tom Uren, created something called the Growth Centres Program, which involved a strategy known as "selective decentralisation," an attempt to concentrate on medium-sized cities rather than spending the money across a lot of projects and towns. The places chosen, as I well remember, were Albury-Wodonga and Bathurst-Orange, though there were some others, including Holsworthy near Sydney and Monarto in South Australia. And the funds were substantial, with the government spending $1 billion in today's money on the growth centres.

Says Paul Collits: "There is little doubt that the Whitlam Government provided the only serious attempt by an Australian government to address what has been perceived historically as Australia's 'regional problem' of unbalanced development and the city-country divide."

But it, too, failed in the end, although Albury-Wodonga remains a solid regional city. Since then, we have seen a succession of regional development policies from both sides of politics, mostly either lip service or money thrown at country electorates for votes, especially by the Coalition, usually either pushed by the National Party or an attempt to offset the rise of Pauline Hanson's One Nation in Queensland. Labor has also had a few goes at it, but through it all Australia's urbanisation has continued to increase steadily, because most people want to live in the cities and because Australia's regional public transport infrastructure is so hopeless. The closest most Australians want to get to the country is a camping trip, the snow or the Gold Coast.

What no government, state or federal, has ever done, is properly invest in fast railway services from regional centres to the cities, so that Australians can live in a country town where the houses are cheap and work in the city. It doesn't even need to be the chimera of the Very Fast Train (VFT) that was talked about in the 1980s, or the High Speed Rail that the Albanese government is now pursuing by setting up a High Speed Rail Authority.

Just reasonably fast, reliable trains that could get from Newcastle to Sydney, or Bendigo to Melbourne, in less than an hour.

The other important element of Australia's extreme urbanisation is that our cities have only one CBD, unlike many others in the world. That means they work as hubs and spokes, and the further from the city you live, the lower the quality of life and the lower the price of the land. As with regional development there have been many attempts to create extra CBDs, the most successful being Chatswood in Sydney, but that's been a limited success. A few collections of high-rise are springing up spontaneously, as in Box Hill and Parramatta, and the Victorian government is planning to build a suburban rail loop that will encircle Melbourne about 20 kilometres from the city, but on the whole Australian cities are focused on the 3 or 4 square kilometres in the middle.

And the thing that turned Australia's hub-and-spoke urbanisation into a housing affordability problem is the car. When cars became affordable for everyone after World War II, it opened up huge tracts of land around the cities for development. This happened everywhere in the world, of course, but two things made it more of a problem here: first, as discussed, each city had just one CBD and second, Australia's cities are relatively new and were not fully developed before the car arrived.

European cities, as well as many in Asia and North America, had been pretty much fully built by the time affordable cars became available, so their design and size were based around public transport, horses and walking. That meant more compact cities, with plenty of medium-density housing. For example, Berlin is one of Europe's largest cities, with 3.9 million people in 892 square kilometres. Melbourne has 5 million people spread over nearly 10,000 square kilometres!

Australia's urban sprawl is notorious around the world, and for good reason. In Melbourne you can drive for 106 kilometres – from Mount Eliza to Kalkallo – and still be in the suburbs. In Europe, that would get you from Rotterdam in the Netherlands to Antwerp in Belgium – another country entirely. My parents were able to buy their block of land in South Oakleigh because they also bought a Vanguard car and didn't have to rely on public transport. And then their children – baby boomers like me – got better cars and sprawled even further out.

Demographer Simon Kuestenmacher tells me that the urban sprawl in Australia is the reason there is little to no medium-density housing, and is entirely due to affordable cars arriving before the cities were fully developed, so that families, including the immigrants from crowded Europe and the United Kingdom, were able to build on large blocks, four or five to an acre. "And once you do that," says Kuestenmacher, "how do you add medium density?"

It's very hard indeed, which brings us to the problem of state and local governments and their control of housing supply through zoning.

SUPPLY PROBLEM 3: STATE AND LOCAL GOVERNMENTS

The Australian constitution is silent on who controls land use — that is, zoning and planning — which means it resides with the states, along with anything else that's not specifically mentioned in the constitution. The state governments delegate most of the work to local councils for three reasons: to ensure that decisions are made closer to the community, to absolve themselves of responsibility and to save money. The problem with this system is that councils are more likely to be corrupt or craven, to be paid off or duchessed by developers, and more unwilling to stand up to the local NIMBYs.

The problem is serious. In March 2018, a couple of economists at the Reserve Bank, Ross Kendall and Peter Tulip, published a paper on the RBA website in which they calculated the impact of zoning on house prices, against both the cost of supply and the actual prices paid. The results were astonishing, and got front-page treatment, along with prominent coverage in TV news bulletins.

After that was published, and because of it, Jason Falinski, the then Liberal member for Mackellar on Sydney's northern beaches, and chair of the Standing Committee on Tax and Revenue, was moved to suggest (yet another) inquiry into housing supply and affordability, and Treasurer Josh Frydenberg agreed to give him a formal referral on 22 July 2021.

Falinski's committee produced its report in March 2022, two months before the 2022 federal election, which the Coalition lost handsomely and in which both Falinski and Frydenberg lost their seats. The report carried the hopeful title of *The Australian Dream*, but because the terms of reference confined it to examining supply — rather than demand as well, which means tax breaks — the Labor members dissented, at length. It now collects dust in the room full of reports in the Parliamentary Library about how to fix Australia's housing crisis, especially now that Labor is in charge.

The findings of Kendall and Tulip in the RBA research report are summarised in this table:

Table 1 *Average house price decomposition: $'000 (per cent of total) 2016*

	Perth	Brisbane	Melbourne	Sydney
Dwelling structure	242 (41)	267 (49)	268 (34)	395 (34)
Land	346 (59)	275 (51)	525 (66)	765 (66)
- Physical land	140 (24)	116 (21)	201 (25)	276 (24)
- Zoning effect	206 (35)	159 (30)	324 (41)	489 (42)
Total	588 (100)	542 (100)	793 (100)	1,160 (100)
Zoning effect as a percentage of physical input costs	54	42	69	73

Source: Ross Kendall and Peter Tulip, The Effect of Zoning on House Prices, Research Discussion Paper 2018–03, Reserve Bank of Australia, 2018.

Another way to look at those numbers is that without zoning, and the restriction on land supply that results from it, houses would be an average of 36.8 per cent cheaper in those four cities. That's not to argue that there should be no zoning of land, but given the impact it has on the price of houses, you would think it should be one of the first ports of call for any attempt to deal with housing affordability.

What is zoning about? Well, in a "primer on zoning and its effects" published a few years ago, the Productivity Commission says:

> Zoning is a way of regulating land use whereby governments divide land into zones (typically using categories such as "industrial", "commercial", "residential" and "mixed") and set rules on how that land may be used. For example, a block of land may be zoned for commercial use, allowing supermarkets and retailers to set up there but prohibiting factories. Governments also use "built form" regulation (that is, rules governing matters such as the construction, height, shape and location of buildings) to shape cities. This is conceptually distinct from land use zoning but, in practice, often forms part of the same set of regulations.

The idea of applying zones to the use of land first developed in the late nineteenth century as a way of governments getting some control over the huge growth in manufacturing industry and urbanisation that occurred after 1880. English common law, which had governed land use up to then, and was transplanted to Australia, wasn't able to stop the growth of nightmarish cities that suited the industrialists who were building the factories and employing the workers, and no one else. In 1909, the Asquith government in the UK brought in the *Housing, Town Planning, etc. Act*, followed by the Zoning Resolution of 1916 in New York City that established height and setback controls and designated residential districts.

Australia followed the UK laws from soon after Federation to 1947, when the Attlee Labour government in Britain introduced a new set of laws and basically nationalised urban planning. The act provided that all development values were vested in the state.

But Australia did not follow suit and stuck with the old laws. As a result, the planning system in Australia never became uniform across the country and was therefore never integrated with housing assistance and the national push for affordable housing as it was in the UK. Subsequent Australian planning laws consider the social, economic and environmental impacts of development, but they have tended to overlay, rather than overturn, existing state government planning schemes.

This has had two important consequences for affordable housing in Australia. First, affordable housing is eroded because local councils aren't responsible for promoting it and require planning proposals to be profitable; and second, when public authorities want to acquire land that's not already set aside or "zoned" for public purposes, they have to pay the market rate, competing with developers.

As a result, any attempts to address housing need through the planning system only happened as a result of piecemeal, local initiatives. As a result, public housing became a marginal and highly targeted form of welfare, shrinking from approximately 18 per cent of total housing stock in 1981 to less than 5 per cent in 2009.

It's tempting to see the post-war development of planning laws in the UK and Australia through the lens of politics: that is, a conservative government was elected a bit earlier after the war in Australia than in the UK (Menzies in 1949 versus Churchill, again, in 1951) and lasted eight years longer (Harold Wilson replaced Alec Douglas-Home in 1964, while the Australian Liberal government was only defeated by Gough Whitlam in 1972).

Yet the truth is Chifley could have reformed Australia's planning laws in 1947 at the same time Attlee did, but he didn't. But it's fair to say that conservative government between 1949 and 1972 on top of Australia's tradition of private-sector housing provision, supplemented by a bit of Commonwealth government-funded public housing, and an ambivalence towards urban regulation, has meant that planning for affordable housing never really happened.

And it turned out that immediately after World War II was the time to reform planning laws, because that's when cars became affordable and everyone got one. As discussed, that's when the great Australian urban sprawl developed and nothing was done to rein it in. Cities consisted of houses on large blocks stretching 20 to 30 kilometres out from the CBD in all directions, with zoning and planning in the hands of local councils elected by the local residents, who became NIMBYs as soon as they moved in. Serious medium density was out. On top of the control exercised by councils, private ownership of individual quarter-acre blocks meant it was impossible for developers to get hold of enough land to build more than four units at a time, and still is.

The result has been that Australian cities have turned into sort of "reverse donuts" – high-rise apartments in and around the CBD and then low-rise (single dwellings) as far as the eye can see, with a few exceptions. Planners and economists call it the "missing middle" and it remains as much of a problem as it was forty years ago.

The blockage represented by Australia's archaic zoning laws is an economic issue that was laid out in pitiless detail by the Reserve Bank economist Tony Richards in an article for the *Australian Financial Review* in March 2023.

The process that a home builder has to go through to take advantage of the demand for medium-density housing and make some money makes it virtually impossible.

The first step would be to go to the website of the local council to check on the rules for new development and the availability of appropriately zoned land in the local government area (LGA). The website would invite the intrepid builder to lodge a development application, unless the project were exempt or complying. To explore this, they would study the council's Local Environment Plan (LEP), a document that is required by state legislation and is typically about 150 pages. In addition, they would have to look at the council's Development Control Plan (DCP), which contains much more detail regarding the development that the council will allow. It may be much longer – hundreds of pages, usually, plus attachments.

Tony Richards goes on:

> The document that will be most relevant for our would-be home builder [apart from the LEP and DCP, presumably] is the zoning map for the LGA. Our builder would no doubt find that there were large swathes of light-pink-coloured R2 (low-density residential) land, which essentially means it can only be used for single-family housing (with some small exceptions for dual-occupancies). And in some Sydney LGAs, there are also significant amounts of land zoned R1 (general residential) or C4 (environmental living), where new building is even more tightly controlled. Other states have different lettering and colours, but it's basically the same.
>
> Our home builder would find much less land zoned for medium-density (R3) or other higher-density or more flexible uses. And they would soon discover that almost all of this land was already being used for medium- or higher-density housing, or was subject to other development proposals. So if our would-be home builder could not find any available land that was already zoned to allow new "missing-middle" housing, how would they go about getting a rezoning?

Rezonings can be one-off (or "spot") rezonings in response to a particular planning proposal, or there may be some broader degree of rezoning around the major update of a council's LEP. These major updates appear to occur about once a decade, after which zoning for the LGA will again be largely set in stone for another decade or so. The process for a spot rezoning is typically a long, difficult and uncertain one, and involves application fees, commissioning costly reports from various subject-matter consultants to support the application and the likely rejection of the application by council. The applicant will then have to decide whether to attempt a costly appeals process that may bring in citywide or state-level bodies.

If a rezoning is eventually achieved, there will then be a long process of negotiating with the council to get development approval for a particular building design. The result is that most would-be home builders are unlikely even to begin – despite the strong demand for medium-density housing.

Instead, says Richards, the way development of medium-density housing often occurs is by developers/speculators trying to anticipate rezoning in future LEPs, possibly a decade or more away. They will then buy up the land, or an option to buy it, and try to influence the council planning process to include their land in a spot rezoning or future LEP. Land banking can be a lucrative proposition in itself, with speculators putting together a group of individual blocks and selling the result to a developer rather than building themselves.

> The upshot is that the important tasks of home building and modernising our cities have become heavily reliant on individuals and companies whose main skill is navigating the development approval process and influencing local and state government officials to try to ease constraints on what can be built.

And now the NIMBYism that characterises most urban planning has led to the emergence of a new movement, called YIMBY – "yes in my backyard." It started in San Francisco about ten years ago, basically because that city's planning laws did not adapt to the employment boom in Silicon Valley that resulted from the technology revolution.

Apparently, a woman stood up at a council meeting in San Francisco waving a courgette and complaining that a development would block sunlight reaching her zucchini garden. The wonderfully named Victoria Fierce stood up and countered: "You're talking about zucchinis? Really? I'm struggling to pay rent!" Ms Fierce went on to become one of the first leaders of the very fierce YIMBY movement.

The first YIMBY group in Australia was set up in the ACT, specifically because of RZ1 – the residential zone that covers about 80 per cent Canberra, specifically all the inner suburbs, and which specifies that housing blocks must have only one dwelling, so medium density is outlawed. It gives Canberra its unique structure of "inner suburban sprawl" and higher density on the outskirts, miles from the city. In other cities it's the other way around.

The Canberra YIMBYs call themselves "GreaterCanberra" and are led by Howard Maclean. They started as a Facebook group talking about the dreadful bus system, but soon moved on to campaigning for an end to RZ1, or at least less of it. They're not partisan, but, as with YIMBYs in the rest of the world, they are mostly millennials, and they have teamed up with the Master Builders Association and the Housing Industry Association, both of which are campaigning for more medium-density housing in Canberra for obvious reasons of their own.

I've been spending some time lately with Jonathan O'Brien, convener of Melbourne's YIMBY group. He started it in October 2022 in, appropriately, the John Curtin Hotel. (Curtin set up the Department of Postwar Reconstruction in 1942, which led to the Commonwealth Housing Commission.) There are also YIMBY groups in Sydney and Brisbane, as well as Canberra, and what they're doing, apart from using social media, writing opinion articles for newspapers and publishing reports, is turning up at local council meetings to argue in favour of medium-density housing.

O'Brien makes the obvious point that the only people speaking at council meetings about development proposals are those who are against them, not in favour, because they're the only ones motivated to turn up. "It's easy to organise against something."

It's early days, and the YIMBY movement is small. In Canberra, where the motivation is the strongest, you'd think, because of the appalling RZ1, there are 100 members of Greater Canberra paying $20 a year ($1 if you're unemployed). Melbourne's group is about the same. ACT chief minister Andrew Barr recently came out in favour of dealing with the "missing middle" of affordable density housing, although he only seemed to be talking about allowing a second dwelling on each block, which is still more low density than medium.

It's baby steps, but starting to build, especially with renters and young voters generally becoming powerful political forces in otherwise conservative electorates such as Kooyong in Melbourne and Wentworth in Sydney.

But while the restrictions on housing supply spearheaded by state and local governments have been a slow burn, and date back decades with failures at all levels of government, the increase in demand that happened around the year 2000 was explosive.

A BRIEF DIVERSION: FANNIE AND FREDDIE

Before we discuss what caused housing demand to increase after 2000, it's worth spending a little more time in the 1930s, looking at something else that happened back then, or rather didn't happen, that's relevant today.

One of the problems facing the Australian economy right now is that a million or so home owners are coming off cheap fixed-rate mortgages onto much more expensive variable rates. It's called the "mortgage cliff" and mainly involves the end of two- and three-year fixed-rate loans during the pandemic at interest rates of around 2 per cent now moving to variable rates of around 7 per cent. On an average mortgage, that's about $2000 a month more. A lot of families will be forced to sell their houses; those who don't will have to cut back other spending and perhaps get a second job.

None of this would be a problem if Australia had thirty-year fixed-rate mortgages, like the United States does. Those who bought at super-low interest rates in 2020–21 would have those low repayments for thirty years or until they sold the house (which they would definitely not do). So why don't we? How come our fixed-rate mortgages max out at five years?

It's because when the Great Depression hit in 1930, Australia had a Labor government, led by Jim Scullin, and the United States had a Republican president, Herbert Hoover. When unemployment goes to 30 per cent for whatever reason, whoever is in power is going to get thrown out, and so it was that Scullin lost the 1932 election to the conservative Joe Lyons, leader of the United Australia Party, and Hoover lost in 1933 to Franklin Delano Roosevelt.

As a result, Australia had a conservative government after the Depression and America had the prince of progressives, FDR. In 1938, as part of his New Deal, Roosevelt created the Federal National Mortgage Association for the specific purpose of providing banks with the guarantees and liquidity they needed to offer thirty-year fixed-rate mortgages; otherwise it would be too risky. The FNMA, later nicknamed Fannie Mae (of course), bought mortgages from the banks and packaged them up for sale to institutional investors looking for solid, property-backed securities. Fannie Mae was later joined by Freddie Mac and Ginnie Mae, and between them these government-sponsored organisations provide the underpinnings of America's unique mortgage system.

Joe Lyons saw what FDR did, but we'll never know whether he would have followed suit because he died in office ten months later and was succeeded by Menzies, who took office three months before war was declared in Europe. The moment was lost.

Why has no subsequent government, Labor or Coalition, set up the Australian equivalent of Fannie, Freddie and Ginnie? I don't know, but I suspect it has something to do with the power of the banks, which do not want to get stuck with thirty-year mortgages.

The restricting of housing supply was a long, slow process, a combination of politics and culture, the child of many parents. Similarly, there isn't one thing that caused demand for housing to take off, although it is easier to pin down in time – that is, from the start of the new millennium. A combination of four things came together to supercharge housing demand and combine with the long-standing supply restrictions to begin Australia's problem with housing affordability.

They are:

1. The Howard government cut capital gains tax by 50 per cent on 23 December 1999.

2. The Howard government resumed paying first home buyer grants on 1 July 2000.

3. The RBA cash rate was cut by 0.5 per cent on 7 February 2001, and then by another 1.5 per cent over the next two years, even though there was no recession in Australia, because of a share market collapse in the United States, which meant that investors rushed from shares to property, funded by cheap debt.

4. Between 2003 and 2009, net migration tripled, but Australia's new open door was not matched by supply of new houses.

1. Capital gains tax and negative gearing

In 1999, Prime Minister John Howard and Treasurer Peter Costello halved the rate of the thirteen-year-old capital gains tax because a panel of three businessmen who were keen on making capital gains themselves recommended it.

The capital gains tax was introduced in 1985 when gains on capital were taxed at the marginal income tax rate of the individual, minus the impact of inflation (that is, the capital gain could be adjusted down by the rise in the consumer price index). On 21 September 1999, the Howard government replaced that CPI adjustment by simply decreeing that only half of any capital gain would be taxable, and since it had just cut income tax rates, this was a double benefit.

That was a big, radical tax reform in itself, but it was Australia's unique system of negative gearing plus the abolition of inheritance taxes twenty years earlier that really made it work. Allowing tax deductions against other income for losses incurred while owning an investment property, and then only taxing half the eventual capital gain at the rate of income tax, and then not taxing inheritances at all made real estate by far the best wealth creation and preservation strategy in Australian history – sustainably better than in the bubble of the 1880s.

As for death duties, as they're called, legend has it that they were killed off in 1978 by Queensland's premier Joh Bjelke-Petersen abolishing inheritance taxes in his state to entice southern retirees to move to Queensland (which they were doing anyway for the weather, and still are). Queensland did do that, but it was Malcolm Fraser who started it by promising to abolish death duties in his election speech in 1977, along with a range of other tax cuts that were totally unnecessary since Whitlam was never going to win in that year after the wipe-out of 1975.

Nevertheless, in his 1977 campaign speech, Fraser said: "Estate duty has caused distress and hardship to thousands of Australian families, to small business, to farmers. Thus, all deceased estates and gifts passing between husband and wife, parent and child, will be exempt from Federal estate and gift duty from this day. Over the life of the next Parliament estate and gift duty will both be entirely abolished." And so they were.

Federal estate and gift duties were first imposed in Australia in 1914, to help finance the war effort. The Estate Duty Assessment Bill introduced by the Fisher Labor government provided for a progressive tax ranging from 1 per cent for estates valued at £1000 to 15 per cent for estates valued £70,000 and over, with a concession for widows, children and grandchildren at two-thirds of normal rates. By 1977 it was 32 per cent for estates above $200,000 and 15 per cent on those from $54,000 to $200,000. In 1979, as promised, these taxes simply evaporated and were not replaced by anything at all. Unsurprisingly, the budget deficit increased because spending wasn't reduced to cover it.

Negative gearing is the term for allowing the deduction of losses on an investment, including interest on any borrowings, from other income, in particular income from labour. Australia's system of allowing unrestricted deductions is unique: many other countries allow a bit of it, but not much, and New Zealand has recently banned it altogether, with no apparent ill effects.

In Australia the argument that abolishing negative gearing would lead to a shortage of rental accommodation doesn't hold water. Apart from anything else, there is currently a dire shortage of rental accommodation with negative gearing in place – hardly an advertisement for its benefits.

But the halving of the capital gains tax in 1999 made it worthwhile to shift income into capital gains wherever possible, because only half of it is taxed if you sell it. And if you don't sell it, none of it is taxed when it passes to your spouse or children when you die. And you get a very handy tax break along the way. Here's how it works ...

A back-of-the-envelope negative gearing calculation
If someone earning $250,000 a year bought that nice little house at 35 Foch Street, Box Hill South, for $1.65 million and borrowed all of that at 6.9 per cent (using the equity in their existing place for the deposit), the repayments would be $11,567 per month, or $138,804 per year. Realestate.com.au tells me it could be rented for $650 a week, or $33,800 a year, so the loss would be a bit more than $105,000 per year. Nasty. Except, that loss would get the investor's taxable income below the $180,000 threshold for the 45 per cent top marginal tax rate, reducing their income tax by about $45,000 a year. The long-term average annual increase in house prices in Melbourne is 7.9 per cent a year; if that capital growth applied to

Box Hill South, as it would, then 35 Foch Street would grow in value, on average, by $130,000 a year, half of which, after inflation, would end up getting taxed at the marginal income tax rate, which is now 37 per cent instead of 45 per cent because of negative gearing, so $24,000 tax per year. If the whole capital gain was taxed at 45 per cent, minus an adjustment for inflation of, say, 3 per cent, that would be $56,745, or $32,745 more. Therefore, with the saving in income tax on top, the investor is $77,745 a year better off than they would have been without Peter Costello's benefaction of 21 September 1999. That represents an investment return, just from the tax benefit, of 4.4 per cent a year ($72,745 as a percentage of the original investment of $1.65 million).

When he announced the halving of the capital gains tax, Treasurer Peter Costello said it was to improve the incentive to invest, which it did, of course, in spades. It's tempting to describe what happened – that house prices took off in relation to incomes and GDP from that moment – as an unintended consequence, but given John Howard's statements that no one ever came up to him complaining that the value of their house had increased too much, maybe it was intended, or at least not unintended. In any case, the context for the decisions that were made in 1999 is important, so we need to delve into that a little.

In those days, politics in Australia was dominated by tax, and also by immigration, thanks to Pauline Hanson, and by the end of 1999 it's fair to say we were all suffering tax reform fatigue. Since the 1985 Tax Summit, and then John Hewson's Fightback! in 1993, Australians had been bombarded with endless debates about tax, culminating on 13 August 1998, when Costello unveiled a white paper titled *A New Tax System*. Two weeks later, Howard announced an early election for 3 October.

That white paper was the product of a taskforce – the "Tax Reform Group" – appointed exactly a year earlier and headed by Ken Henry, then secretary of the Treasury, and including a bunch of other senior public servants. Their instructions were that there should be no overall increase in the tax burden, there should be "major reductions in personal income tax," and "consideration should be given to a broad based, indirect tax to replace some or all of the existing indirect taxes."

Howard had ruled out a GST in 1995 ahead of the 1996 election that brought him to power ("never ever," is what he said), after his predecessor, John Hewson, lost to Paul Keating in 1993 because of his plan for a GST, but once Howard and Costello were in government Treasury told them there had to be one. No way out of it. So, the purpose of Henry's Tax Reform Group was to provide the justification for a 10 per cent goods and services tax, plus a series of income tax cuts to offset it. Armed with their report, Howard announced that there would be a GST, to be introduced after the 1998 election, which he then won – just – losing fourteen seats, a two-party-preferred vote of just 49 per cent and without control of the Senate. As a result, he had to negotiate the GST at some length with the Democrats, led by Meg Lees.

Within three weeks of the election, and while all this discussion about GST was going on, Costello quietly announced a review of business taxation to be chaired by John Ralph, a former CEO of Rio Tinto who was then president of the Business Council of Australia and also chairman of Foster's and Pacific Dunlop, as well as a director of the Commonwealth Bank, Telstra and BHP (phew). A few months earlier, Howard had hosted Ralph for dinner at the Lodge with the new president of the Business Council, Stan Wallis, and the two business leaders urged the prime minister to cut company tax, as you do if you're a leading company director having dinner with the PM – while saying that it's in the national interest, of course.

Ralph was joined on the Review of Business Taxation panel by Rick Allert, a director of five companies, and Bob Joss, who was in the process of stepping down as managing director of Westpac Bank to become Dean of the Graduate School of Management at Stanford, in the United States. Their terms of reference mainly directed them to look at "the goal of moving towards a 30 per cent company tax rate" (from 36 per cent), which – surprise, surprise! – the three company directors thought was a terrific idea and recommended doing as soon as possible, please.

The terms of reference also asked them to look at "capping the rate of capital gains applying to individuals at 30 per cent," but they decided to go further than that. The three businessmen tasked with redesigning business taxes recommended – another surprise! – that only 50 per cent of the capital gains on assets held for a year or more be included in the taxable income of an individual, to "help support a strong investment culture among Australian households."

And so it did when Howard and Costello adopted it, although perhaps not the investments intended. Ralph, Allert and Joss had in mind that Australian households would be motivated to invest in company shares and lower their cost of capital. They didn't: the investment culture among Australian households was all about real estate, and had been for 100 years, and so it remained.

Labor MP Mark Latham, then a backbencher, is recorded in Hansard as saying in a speech on 24 November 1999:

> Some say the inequities in the [capital gains tax] package will be offset by the abolition of indexation. They must have come down in the last shower, because the only reason indexation is being abolished is that inflation is so low and there is barely anything left to index with.
>
> While some might say the GST is going to lift inflation – and most certainly it will – we all know it is an undesirable but yet one-off impact. I wish the capital gains tax halving was just a one-off, but once this thing is in the statute books it will be pretty hard to get out. If you let the white shoes put their foot in the door, we all know how hard it is to get them out. This will be anything but a one-off effect on the Australian economy.

Latham was wrong about one thing (he's been wrong about a few things since then): it wasn't just the white shoes (spivs and chancers) who put their foot in the door – it was everyone. That's because the halving of CGT was the kerosene on the smouldering coals of negative gearing and the lack of an inheritance tax, and turned property investing from a niche activity into the leaping flame of everybody's tax avoidance scheme.

Before December 1999, the number of rental properties incurring a loss was roughly the same as the number making a capital profit, but after that the losses ballooned, as shown by Figure 7, produced in 2016 by the Grattan Institute.

The words "negative gearing" didn't make it into the report from John Ralph, Rick Allert and Bob Joss recommending the halving of capital gains tax, but that was the thing that turned what seemed like a good idea at the time (for businesspeople like them) into a disaster for housing affordability.

Some background on negative gearing is warranted. Australian taxpayers have (almost) always been allowed to deduct investment losses from their other income, although it became more controversial in the mid-1980s after the "bottom of the harbour" schemes focused national attention on tax avoidance. In 1983, the Victorian Deputy Commissioner of Taxation briefly denied real estate investors the deduction for interest in excess of the rental income, but he was quickly overruled by the federal tax commissioner. Then, after the tax summit held in July 1985 amid a flurry of efforts to stop tax avoidance, the Hawke government banned negative gearing entirely, disallowing the deduction of interest expenses on properties bought after 17 July 1985. It meant that taxpayers could only offset interest expenses against rental income.

Announcing the change, Treasurer Paul Keating said:

> The Leader of the Opposition would allow all the high-income earners to run interest costs against their income, swapping flats on Bondi Beach which were built 40 years ago. That is not adding to the stock of housing or to the stock of rental accommodation, it is not really assisting families who need rental accommodation. We have wiped out that outrageous rort and introduced accelerated depreciation for new buildings or major renovations in order to create more rental property and more opportunities for renters.

Figure 7 Since the introduction of the capital gains tax discount, rental losses have been large

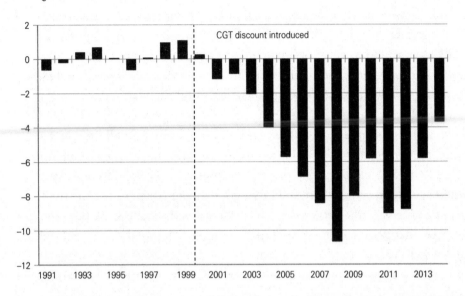

Source: Grattan Institute, ATO.

There was an outcry from the powerful property industry and rents in Sydney did increase, quite a lot, but that was for reasons other than the abolition of negative gearing. Nevertheless, in 1987 Hawke caved in and reinstated negative gearing, while arguing that the introduction of capital gains tax in 1985 had made that reversal okay. And that's probably true, since the use of negative gearing didn't really take off and make housing unaffordable until CGT was halved by Howard and Costello in December 1999.

The combination of those two decisions – reinstatement of negative gearing in 1987 and halving the CGT in 1999 – has meant that whereas in the rest of the world investing in real estate is all about getting rental income from tenants, in Australia it's about getting an income tax deduction and then a capital gain.

It produces a totally different investment motivation and has produced a fundamentally different approach to housing in Australia than in most other places. And as an aside, that's also why institutions don't invest in residential property in Australia, unlike in the rest of the world, where they do – they don't get the tax deduction. In the United States, institutions "build to rent" – that is, they build residential property, usually apartment blocks, with the intention of holding them and renting them out. In Australia there is virtually no "build to rent," it's all about developers building to sell to individual negative gearers, preferably off the plan.

For a decade and a half, the arguments about negative gearing bubbled away in opinion pieces and think-tank papers, and eventually reached a crescendo on Saturday, 12 February 2016. On that day, the leader of the Labor Party, Bill Shorten, got a standing ovation at the NSW ALP conference when he announced that a future Labor government would restrict negative gearing to new homes and halve the capital gains discount to 25 per cent. He took that policy to the 2016 federal election five months later and did pretty well: Labor won fourteen seats off the Coalition, reducing the government to a majority of just one, having lost heavily three years earlier, with a swing of 3.1 per cent.

Emboldened, Shorten doubled down. He went to the 2019 election against Scott Morrison with the same tax policies and added a crackdown on dividend franking for good measure. Before the election the bookies had Labor as the favourite to win and Shorten was starting to think about new curtains in the Lodge. In the event, though, he lost badly, with a swing against him of 1.2 per cent and the net loss of one seat. Morrison was triumphant; Shorten was dumped as leader in favour of Anthony Albanese.

Was it dividend franking or negative gearing that lost the 2019 election for Labor? It was probably both, but mainly dividend franking I'd say. However, Shorten's real problem was his spending promises. A review for Labor of the election by Craig Emerson and Jay Weatherill was inconclusive about the impact of the tax increases, but noted that, "Going into an election campaign with unfunded expenditure of more than $100 billion would have exposed Labor to a highly effective attack of massively increasing budget deficits and debt." To pay for those promises Shorten had to increase taxes, and he thought negative gearing, capital gains and dividend franking would be the least unpopular.

The fact that he was completely wrong says a lot about how deeply embedded in Australian society property speculation had become, and how important dividend income had become for self-funded retirees. In 2022, Labor with Albanese as leader went to the election promising no new spending and no new taxes, or any changes to the tax system at all, and won handsomely. It took less than twelve months for that promise to be broken with an extra tax on superannuation.

Would a Labor victory in 2016, with negative gearing being confined to new properties and the capital gains tax discount halved from 50 to 25 per cent, have changed the course of house prices and ended the affordability crisis? It's impossible to know, of course, and tax concessions are just one of many factors affecting house prices in this country. But since 2016 the median capital city house price in Australia has gone from $550,000 to $716,000, a rise of 30 per cent, while the average wage has increased by 19 per cent. You would think that had Shorten won in 2016, that might not have happened to the same extent, and the median house price might only have increased 19 per cent.

2. First home buyer grants

In his 2013 submission to one of the many parliamentary inquiries into housing affordability, Saul Eslake wrote: "It's hard to think of any government policy that has been pursued for so long, in the face of such incontrovertible evidence that it doesn't work, than the policy of giving cash to first home buyers in the belief that doing so will promote home ownership."

The practice started in 1964, when Bob Menzies started dishing out cash grants to first home buyers at the urging of the NSW Division of the Young Liberals, whose president was a 25-year-old John Howard, then a junior solicitor with Stephen, Jaques and Stephen. As a result of Howard's lobbying, the Menzies government paid Home Savings Grants of up to $500 to "married or engaged couples under the age of 36" on the basis of $1 for every $3 saved in an "approved form" (that is, in a bank) in the three years prior to buying their first home, provided that the home was valued at no more than $14,000.

Gough Whitlam abolished that scheme in 1973, in favour of a tax deduction of interest for anyone earning less than $14,000. It was reintroduced by Malcolm Fraser in 1976 without the age or marriage requirements or the value limits, and with a larger maximum grant of $2500, replaced by the Hawke government in 1983 as the First Home Owners Assistance Scheme, initially with a maximum grant of $7000 (later reduced to $6000) and subject to an income test; then it was abolished again in 1990 by Paul Keating.

It remained abolished for ten years, until 1 July 2000, when the Howard government introduced the First Home Owners Grant (FHOG) without any income test or upper limit on the purchase price of homes acquired, as part of the "compensation" for the introduction of the GST, even though, as Eslake pointed out, the GST only applied to the purchase of new homes and not to existing dwellings, which the majority of first-time buyers purchase.

Since then, there has been a steady flow of first home buyer schemes, including Kevin Rudd's huge First Home Owners Boost in 2008, in the midst of the GFC, designed to boost construction. It doubled the existing grant from $7000 to $14,000 and gave first home buyers who bought a newly constructed home an extra $14,000 to take their grant to $21,000. Most states and territories also had their own first home buyer schemes, so that in his 2013 submission Eslake estimated that the total amount of money outlaid by governments on these schemes between 1964 and 2011 was $22.5 billion in 2010/11 dollar values. It would be a lot more now.

Cash grants to first home buyers are political attempts to appear to be doing something while making things worse. They do help some individuals, of course, but at a macro level they achieve the opposite of helping. As Eslake pointed out, assistance to first-time home buyers has "served simply to exacerbate the already substantial imbalance between the underlying demand for housing and the supply of it."

3. Interest rates and the sharemarket bust

Global share prices peaked in March 2000 and fell 50 per cent over the next two years, thanks mainly to an 80 per cent crash by the American technology index, called the Nasdaq. This was the unwinding of the dotcom bubble of the 1990s, one of the greatest speculative manias in history. Australian shares fared relatively better, because we didn't, and still don't, have much in the way of technology companies; the share market is dominated by banks and mining companies, not tech stocks. So while the Nasdaq was shooting skywards during the 1990s – going up tenfold from 1 January 1990 to 24 March 2000, in all the irrational exuberance about the internet – the Australian All Ordinaries index only went up 87 per cent.

After the bust there was a global bear market (a decline in share prices) in the first few years of the new millennium and despite not having many tech stocks, Australia got caught up to some extent – our market declined by one-eighth between 2000 and 2003. The United States went into recession in March 2001 and Europe also had a brief recession from the end of that year. Australia avoided recession, even though the Reserve Bank, then led by Governor Ian Macfarlane, had been unwisely hiking interest rates into the global storm, including three rate hikes in 2000 after the dotcom bust had happened. The RBA cash rate – which is the overnight rate banks charge each other, and is the one the RBA influences – went from 4.75 per cent at the start of November 1999 to 6.25 per cent in August 2000, even though the US share market had been crashing for five months at that point and it was clear that a lot of trouble was brewing.

So the Reserve Bank had to hurriedly reverse course and in February 2001 it cut interest rates by 0.5 per cent, following by 0.25 per cent in March and 0.5 per cent in April. By February 2002, the cash rate was back down to 4.25 per cent.

All of which prompted a flight of investors from shares to property in 2000/01, which became a stampede because of the halving of capital gains tax in December 1999. The value of share transactions fell 10 per cent, while

Figure 8 Established house price index and CPI (base year: 1986 = 100)

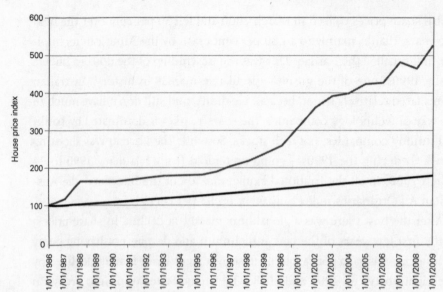

Source: Department of Parliamentary Services.

the value of real estate transactions increased 17.5 per cent. By the middle of 2002, when interest rates started rising again, loans to housing investors were growing at more than 20 per cent a year, and in 2003 hit 30 per cent.

As a result, house prices started trending sharply higher, having earlier been given a solid boost from 1996 by a quick series of five 0.5 per cent rate cuts.

And because of that, the house price-to-income ratio jumped from about 3.5 to 5, and household debt went from 90 per cent of income to 150 per cent in just a few years.

At the same time, share prices headed south.

After 2003, the rush out of shares and into property faded. House prices stabilised at the new, higher level, and another one of the great share market rises in history got underway, before coming to a very sticky end in 2007 because of the US housing bust, which led to the banking crunch and global financial crisis of 2008. That led, in turn, to another series of dramatic interest rate cuts and, inevitably, to another boom in house prices. The

Figure 9 Debt- and price-to-income ratios

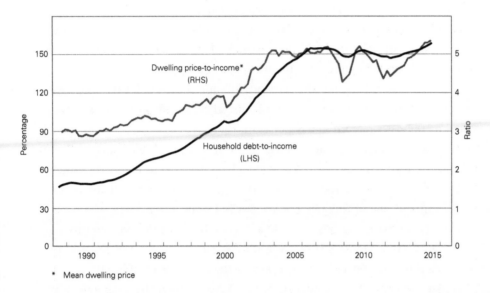

* Mean dwelling price

Sources: ABS, CoreLogic RP Data, RBA.

median price in Sydney rose 68 per cent between 2010 and the pandemic of 2020, and in Melbourne by 54 per cent.

Now we need to talk about the inflation target. The Reserve Bank started targeting a certain inflation rate in the early 1990s. There was never a formal announcement, but it's usually dated to March 1993, when the RBA governor, Bernie Fraser, said in a speech that keeping inflation between 2 and 3 per cent might be a good outcome. He said it a few more times, then treasurer Paul Keating and ACTU secretary Bill Kelty included it in the final Accord in 1995, and then it was formalised when the new treasurer, Peter Costello, signed a Statement on the Conduct of Monetary Policy in 1996 with the incoming governor of the RBA, Ian Macfarlane.

Whenever it started, and whoever thought of it, the 2 to 3 per cent inflation target has been a disaster for housing in Australia. That's because when inflation fell below 2 per cent at the beginning of 2015, and stayed there, the Reserve Bank was obliged to try to get it up. The cash rate had already been cut to 2.5 per cent and had been sitting at that level for eighteen months, but in 2015 it was cut to 2 per cent and then a year later to 1.5 per cent, where it stayed for nearly three years. And then, unbelievably, between June and October 2019, the RBA under Philip Lowe's leadership cut interest rates three more times – to 0.75 per cent – in an effort to get inflation *up* to 2 per cent.

Those five years between the start of 2015 and the end of 2019 were one of the worst periods in the history of Australian housing. In the first two years, as the cash rate sat at 1.5 per cent, there was a property investment boom that prompted the intervention of the Australian Prudential and Regulatory Authority. APRA cracked down on bank lending to investors, which had got quite out of control, and the boom came to a sudden end and house prices suffered one of their biggest ever falls (about 9 per cent).

The RBA's inflation target soon put a stop to that with those three further rate cuts in 2019. House prices were on the move again – not because of investors this time, but owner-occupiers using cheap loans to bid up prices.

When the COVID-19 pandemic hit in March 2020, the cash rate was 0.75 per cent, and a panicking RBA had very little room to move. It quickly cut the cash rate to 0.1 per cent but felt that wasn't enough in what seemed to be an existential economic threat. Which is why Lowe started saying that the RBA didn't expect interest rates to be increased until 2024. That "expectation" about interest rates staying where they were was taken to be a promise.

Specifically, home owners thought a three-year fixed-rate mortgage would be fine because the variable rate would still be low when it ended. Nothing could be further from the truth, as it turned out, because in 2022, the 2 to 3 per cent inflation target worked dramatically the other way when post-pandemic inflation soared to more than 7 per cent.

When Bernie Fraser first brought in the target, inflation had averaged 8.7 per cent over the previous twenty years, and it was all about ensuring that inflation didn't go above 3 per cent and get embedded in expectations and wage claims, so that a spiral developed. But when it resulted in the cash rate being cut to 1.5 per cent and then 0.75 per cent to get inflation *above* the bottom of the target range, it was both disastrous and absurd.

Disastrous because of the way it distorted decision-making and house prices, and absurd because an inflation rate of 1 to 2 per cent, as it was, is not dangerous in the way an inflation rate of 5 to 6 per cent can be. It simply means prices are not rising very much. Big deal. Deflation – falling prices – can be dangerous because it discourages spending (people tend to wait for things to get cheaper and also debt gets relatively larger), but inflation that's just below 2 per cent is not an actual problem. But the Reserve Bank treated its target as a commandment – that inflation had to be between 2 and 3 per cent.

4. Immigration

Between 1948 and 2003, net overseas migration into Australia averaged 90,890 per year. After that it surged to a peak of 299,870 in 2009, with the biggest increase between 2005 and 2007, when the number of migrants coming into Australia went from 123,760 to 232,800 in two years. As a result of the step-change that took place in the mid-2000s, net overseas migration averaged 214,560 between 2005 and 2020, more than double the average of the previous fifty years.

That increase was never announced by the government as an intention, and it was never taken to an election. In fact, it looked for all the world like the opposite was happening – that Australia was pulling up the drawbridge. The quiet, massive increase in immigration coincided with the clampdown on refugees following the incident in August 2001 when the Norwegian con-tainer vessel MV *Tampa*, with 433 Afghan Hazaras on board, was refused entry into Australian waters, and John Howard famously declared, "We will decide who comes to this country and the circumstances in which they come."

The increase in immigration under Howard was part of his industrial relations strategy to crush unions and suppress wage growth, and the crack-down on refugees was deliberately designed to cover it – to make it look like the opposite was happening. Howard's IR plans began as soon as he was elected, with the *Workplace Relations Act 1996*, and culminated in the *Workplace Relations Amendment Act 2005*, also known as WorkChoices, which turned out to be an overreach and helped cost him the 2007 election.

Figure 10 Net overseas migration – Australia – historical

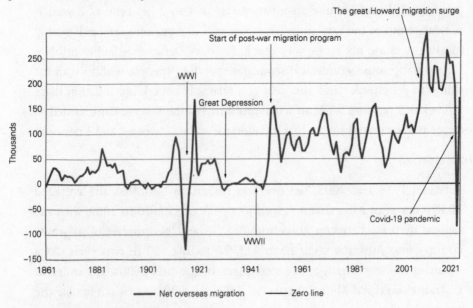

Source: ABS.

In between those bookends was the waterfront dispute of 1998, in which the Howard government supported Patrick Stevedores' successful effort to sideline the Maritime Union, and the creation of the Australian Building and Construction Commission in 2005, set up to investigate and prosecute building unions. Unions generally were already on the ropes as a result of enterprise bargaining, and Howard delivered the coup de grâce by cutting their funding and making it harder for them to get legal representation.

So the loud crackdown on refugees provided cover for the quiet, unannounced but much more significant increase in legal immigration designed to support Howard's work in reducing the power of unions and workers. And it worked, but only after Howard was gone. Wage growth collapsed from 4.2 per cent to 1.2 per cent between the 2007 election and 2021, and trade union membership, already in decline, halved from 24 per cent to 12.5 per cent.

Figure 11 Home construction versus population growth

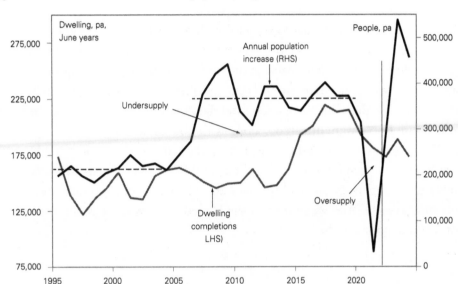

Source: AMP.

But, of course, the other consequence of Howard's surge in immigration was a shortage of housing, because no thought was given at all to where the new arrivals might live. As population increased, housing construction stayed the same, and didn't increase until the late 2010s.

Net migration averaging about 200,000 a year for twenty years has seen Australia's population grow by 7.2 million, from 19.5 to 26.7 million between 2003 and 2023, but the total number of dwellings has increased by only 3 million, from 7.2 to 10.2 million. Assuming two people per dwelling, on average, that leaves a shortfall of 1.2 million houses.

That population growth has produced average growth in GDP of 2.4 per cent a year, much more than per capita GDP growth, which has been just 0.8 per cent a year. Meanwhile, company profits have grown by an average of 8.4 per cent a year over the past fifteen years and the number of billionaires has increased at a compound annual growth rate of 6 per cent. But wages have grown half as much as prices over that period – 6.7 per cent versus 13.1 per cent.

In other words, the failure to support the high level of immigration with enough accommodation has worsened inequality by suppressing real wages and making housing unaffordable at the same time. So population growth, along with tax breaks, interest rate cuts and first home buyer grants, produces some winners but more losers, and the losers lose big, because of the way house prices were driven up, along with household debt.

Those boosts to demand engineered by the federal government might not have been such a problem if the state and local governments had kept up housing supply, but they didn't, and now the whole of Australian society must wear it. And we've seen in the United States what large numbers of working poor can do.

SOLUTIONS

In his farewell speech in September 2023, the outgoing governor of the Reserve Bank, Philip Lowe, said:

> the reason that Australia has some of the highest housing prices in the world ... is the outcome of the choices we have made as a society: choices about where we live; how we design our cities, and zone and regulate urban land; how we invest in and design transport systems; and how we tax land and housing investment. In each of these areas, our society and politicians have made choices that lead to high urban land and housing costs. It is by tackling these issues that we can address the high cost of housing in Australia, which I view as a serious economic and social problem.

That is a pretty full list of the reasons for the high cost of housing in Australia, and a succinct statement from a serious economist that it's a problem that needs to be addressed. But Liberal MP Jason Falinski got one thing right in his report on housing in 2022: there are two tribes when it comes to thinking about the solution to unaffordable housing. One tribe says the problem is tax breaks that boost demand too much and the other says it's zoning and planning that restrict supply. The two tribes, he said, can't be reconciled.

And the report of the Parliamentary Standing Committee on Tax and Revenue that Falinski chaired, titled *The Australian Dream: Inquiry into housing affordability and supply in Australia*, became just another display of the tribalism. The Coalition-dominated majority report was tribe 2 (supply) and the dissenting report from Labor members was tribe 1 (demand), in which they complained that the report's focus was all about supply.

That report dropped two months before Labor won the 2022 election, so you'd think the new government would be in tribe 1, focused on demand and taxes, in line with Labor's dissenting report. But while there has since been a flurry of activity on housing, it's all been about supply. None of the work now going on is aimed at negative gearing or capital gains tax, for the simple reason that, politically, tax is toxic, to be avoided like the plague.

There is some talk about replacing stamp duty with land tax, but it's not serious and it wouldn't make any difference to the underlying issue of affordability if it happened. And there is also some talk of tax incentives for "build to rent," which might help the rental crisis if institutions could be persuaded or bribed to build apartment towers and rent them out. But all that would do is offset the tax advantage that individual owners get from negative gearing and capital gains tax, which is unavailable to institutions and is the reason Australia doesn't do build to rent – since tax-advantaged individuals outbid institutions.

The housing activity in this term of government began with Labor's election promise to build 30,000 homes over five years, with $10 billion capital put into something called the Housing Australia Future Fund, which would be managed by the Future Fund and would distribute the annual returns to states so they could build public or social houses with the income. The 30,000 houses – 6000 a year – is a guess based on what the returns might be and what the houses might cost. Then, as we have seen, in 2022 there was a National Cabinet agreement for an "aspirational target" of 1 million houses over five years through more land release, and that was upped to 1.2 million in 2023 with the offer of $15,000 bounties, per block, paid by the federal government to states, capped at $3 billion.

And now the federal housing minister, Julie Collins, has launched a consultation process to develop a National Housing and Homelessness Plan. If the process does turn into a plan, it will be the first since 1946. Since then, the federal government has never taken responsibility for developing a national plan, so the federal–state accords in 2022 and 2023 aimed at increasing supply and Collins' work on a plan are potentially groundbreaking.

But the issues paper Collins put out in August does not mention the impact of tax on the demand for housing, or rather it is only mentioned in the context of stamp duty or tax incentives for build-to-rent accommodation. Here are the seven areas listed in the paper for discussion and feedback:

homelessness, homelessness services, Aboriginal and Torres Strait Islander housing, social housing, housing costs, home ownership and the rental market in Australia, planning, zoning and development and the impact of climate change and disasters on housing security, sustainability and health.

All of these are worthwhile, but this project is within the Department of Social Services, so the government is coming at it as a welfare issue rather than an economic one.

Before we get into specific solutions to Australia's housing problem, and try to reconcile the tribes, I think we need to take a step back. Why has nothing ever worked? Why has a succession of inquiries and reports, along with a museum full of academic papers and journalism on the subject, never led to serious, effective action to improve housing affordability?

In my view it's because all the work has been both aimless and unsupported by a national consensus. Solutions by the dozen have been proposed to increase the supply of dwellings through better zoning and planning and/or to reduce demand, usually by knocking off one or more tax breaks. But what's the aim, exactly? And more importantly, what's the real national mood, and therefore the politics?

The politics of it is both simple and difficult: housing is a cartel of the majority, with banks and developers helping them maintain high house prices with the political class actively supporting them.

Everybody involved in this game – home owners, banks, property developers and state and federal politicians – wants house prices to rise for their own reasons. Renters don't stand a chance.

Australia's 27 million people live in 10.8 million dwellings, of which 65 per cent are owned and 35 per cent are rented. That is the lowest rate of home ownership in 20 years, but it's still a big majority. Two-thirds of the population is therefore in favour of restricting the supply of houses to maintain the value of their own and they are supported in that by banks and developers.

Banks make more profit as higher house prices increase their assets and interest income, developers make more money if the price of their product is high, state governments make more stamp duty, and greater wealth supports the national economy and keeps federal politicians in power.

It means that any genuine attempt to deal with housing affordability and the shortage of rental accommodation would have to contradict the interests of both the majority of citizens and those with the most power. There is lip service paid to the problem of affordability and "promises" to build a certain number of houses to ease it, but these are usually not fulfilled, and are never actual promises to build anything, just aspirational forecasts – like the latest one from the Albanese government to "build" 1.2 million houses over five years.

I'll get to that in a moment, but first, if there is ever going to be a housing policy that means anything, it needs to have an explicit aim. All the work on this subject, including the latest project being led by Julie Collins, is like a journey with no destination. What are we trying to achieve? And does anyone who matters really want to achieve it?

In my view, the aim should be simple and easily stated and understood, and should refer to the problem identified at the start of this essay: that the price of housing is now twice the multiple of income it used to be. It was three to four times average weekly earnings, now it's seven to eight times. Any serious effort to deal with housing affordability should be explicitly aimed at getting that ratio down and keeping it there.

Expressing that as the aim of policy and then providing leadership towards a national consensus around it must be the start of any genuine plan. Any government policy also needs to acknowledge that the two most important factors in housing affordability have little to do with housing, and won't ever be part of any housing policy: interest rates and bank regulation.

Only two things have ever resulted in a (temporary) improvement in housing affordability: higher interest rates and, in 2016–17, a crackdown on bank lending to real estate investors. But neither of those things was aimed at improving the affordability of housing; interest rates rise and fall according to what the Reserve Bank thinks the economy needs, and the Australian Prudential Regulatory Authority is concerned with the stability of the financial system. Neither has a mandate to do anything about the price of houses and their actions won't be influenced by any government policy designed to improve housing affordability.

But perhaps there's an even more fundamental bridge that needs to be crossed before we look at solutions: is the big rise in house prices since 2000 good or bad? Economists refer approvingly to a "wealth effect," and Australia has had that in spades: per capita wealth has increased fivefold in thirty years. Whenever the ABS releases the latest survey of wealth, I get reports from economists writing that it's a very good thing. The economy has got stronger due to the increase in wealth and the majority of Australians are happier.

The value of other assets – shares, infrastructure and commercial property – has also been increasing more rapidly than incomes, but that is unequivocally a good thing, except when it gets out of control and turns into a bubble that bursts. Superannuation accounts, mostly without residential property, have been increasing at a clip of about 9 per cent per annum, about three times the rate of wage growth, and any fund that only manages to return the rate of wage growth is likely to go out of business.

The difference with housing, of course, is that it's also where you live, and as a result there are losers as well as winners with high and rising prices. And while the winners outnumber the losers two to one, and in a democracy that would normally be the end of the matter, sometimes the right thing for a society isn't necessarily what the majority wants. Many people, myself included, used to enjoy smoking, but governments decided it was bad for society and worked on cutting it back through advertising bans, labelling and taxes.

Half of Australia's home owners are locked in a wealth-creation partnership with a bank. Real estate is such an effective accumulator of wealth because you can borrow at least 80 per cent of the value, often more, and the leverage means that every dollar you invest is multiplied fivefold when the price increases. That's usually a risky, speculative thing to do in investing, but with real estate it's safe because there aren't 50 per cent crashes in residential property as there are on the share market about every ten years, or not for 130 years anyway, so banks are happy to lend much more than they are with shares. And bank executives build their wealth alongside their customers; they are not only very keen to lend against housing but also keen to make sure that house prices keep rising.

It's not just the house-owning majority who think about housing as wealth-creation as well as, or even instead of, shelter – everybody regards housing as an appreciating asset. Renters talk about getting on the "property ladder"; they'd prefer it to be easier to get on, but they want it to be a ladder once they're on it. We're all so used to house prices always rising that it's hard to imagine life any other way.

And the biggest tax dodge of all, of course, is that if you live in the house there is no capital gains tax at all. I know families that have grown their wealth by moving every two to five years, buying, renovating and selling for a tax-free capital gain. Tough on the kids and their schooling, but it works a treat!

So the number one blockage to dealing with housing affordability is that there is no consensus that there is a problem at all, let alone how to fix it. Academics, economists and journalists all say it's a crisis, and millennial renters complain bitterly because they cannot buy a house, but the majority of home-owning Australians are happy to shut up and keep growing their wealth – and banks, developers and governments are all happy to make sure it happens.

My view, and the basis of this essay, is that there definitely is a problem and that the high price of housing is undermining social cohesion and the proper functioning of the economy and the nation. The doubling of house prices in relation to incomes has distorted Australian society over the past twenty-five years and focused wealth creation on an unproductive asset. Something must be done about it even though most people may not like it.

Moreover, there is no point making a small change, say by trying to keep the housing-to-income ratio where it is, or down from the current seven to eight times average weekly earnings to six to seven times, or even five to six times. To achieve anything in life you have to aim high. If there is to be a genuine effort to improve housing affordability, the aim must be to return the ratio to three to four times average weekly earnings, as it was twenty-five years ago.

The latest national median house price is $740,668. The current average full-time adult wage is $1,907.20 per week, or $99,174.40 a year – call it $100,000. For the house price-to-income ratio to be what it was twenty-five years ago, the national median price would have to halve, to $370,000. But that's not going to happen, of course, and it wouldn't be a good idea even if it could. Even if the government could pull that off, which it couldn't, there'd be a riot and, as there was in the United States in 2007/08, an economic collapse.

More realistically, house prices need to stay put for a while and allow incomes to catch up. Average weekly earnings are currently rising at about 4 per cent a year. For the national median house price of $740,668 to be 3.5 times income, the average wage would have to be $210,000, more than double what it is now. At 4 per cent growth in incomes per year, that would take about eighteen years.

The only time house prices remained unchanged for that long was from 1930 to 1949 – that is, during the Great Depression and the period of price controls in the war. Even after the recessions of 1982 and 1991, it took less than half that long for prices to start rising again.

So fifteen to twenty years of static house prices would be unprecedented, but that sort of time frame might also get Australians out of the habit of thinking that house prices always rise and that housing is the best way to build wealth. And if housing affordability is to be properly dealt with, we have to change that mindset, because house prices won't stop rising at twice the rate of incomes unless we stop expecting them to.

If the government were serious about housing affordability, it would announce an affordability target like the one that I am suggesting, of something like three to four times average incomes, and would say: "We're going to achieve that target by doing everything we can to ensure that house prices stay where they are for eighteen years, to allow incomes to catch up."

So how would that be done? It's easy: by ensuring that there was enough supply to meet demand, and since it's probably working against two enormously powerful forces that are doing their own thing – monetary policy and bank marketing – that means both sides of the equation, demand and supply, must be pressed into service, not just one of the two tribes. And every tool in the shed must be put to work.

The first thing you would do is stop the tax system from distorting demand by limiting negative gearing to newly built houses, and by cutting the capital gains discount to 25 per cent, as the ALP wanted to do in 2016 and 2019, and seems to have vowed never again to mention, let alone do. Alternatively, capital gains tax could be returned to what it was between 1985 and 1999 – that is, adjusting the gain for inflation before taxing it at the marginal income tax rate.

The second action on demand should be to link immigration to the capacity of the Australian construction industry – specifically, net overseas migration would be kept at roughly two to two-and-a-half times the number of housing approvals, forever. This should include a clear assessment of the infrastructure needs of population growth as well – harder to figure out, but not impossible. Immigration policy should not simply be driven by the demand for labour.

There is more or less constant pressure from businesses and their lobby groups for higher levels of immigration, especially at the moment because of staff shortages, but at other times to keep wages down, but this should be explicitly and firmly tied to housing and infrastructure. Every two migrants must be matched with a house.

It's clear that suppressing demand for housing by increasing taxes is difficult. Those tax policies arguably cost the ALP two elections, and political will on the subject has been drained away. And linking immigration to housing approvals requires the sort of courageous and imaginative approach to the labour market and to federal–state relations that seems beyond today's politicians.

So it's probably true that most of the effort needs to go into increasing the supply of houses. That is certainly the approach of most academic work, the Collins national plan project and the Falinski inquiry, which was called the "Inquiry into housing affordability and supply in Australia," with no mention of demand in the terms of reference at all.

The key recommendation was to "provide incentive payments to state and local governments to encourage the adoption of better planning and property administration policies." That was picked up by this year's National Cabinet plan to pay $15,000 per land release to state and local governments – without acknowledgement, of course, since that would involve admitting that something the other tribe had thought of was a good idea.

But those payments are capped at $3 billion over five years – 200,000 dwellings in total, or 40,000 a year. The other million of the Albanese "promise" of 1.2 million houses is simply best endeavours, aka pie in the sky.

Demographer Simon Kuestenmacher proposes a stick rather than a carrot: that is, give every local council a quota of medium-density housing approvals and if the councillors don't meet it, take money away from them. And if they don't meet it for two years in a row, sack them. That would certainly focus minds.

Pressure on councils, whether carrot or stick, must be part of the solution, but not just any councils. The essence of the problem of affordability is location. Land that's further than 50 kilometres from the city is cheap and councils there are happy to approve more housing, but it's useless if there are no jobs, shops, doctors or public transport. The need is for more housing close to the city, or infrastructure, and that means the NIMBYs must be overruled by the councils they elected.

In a recent article in Inside Story, Peter Mares wrote that between the 2011 and 2021 censuses, dwelling supply in Melbourne's nine inner-city councils increased by about a third. In the City of Melbourne, housing supply almost doubled in that time, from 53,000 to 103,000 dwellings, as new high-rise residential towers sprouted up across the Hoddle grid, Southbank and Docklands. The supply of housing on the urban fringe rose by more than 50 per cent over the decade, mostly in the form of detached housing in residential developments on former farmland.

But the supply of housing in Melbourne's middle- and outer-ring suburbs grew by just 13 per cent. That's the "well-located" suburbs, close to transport, hospitals, supermarkets and other amenities.

But as Mares says, the problem isn't mainly councils blocking development, it's that there aren't a lot of sites available for developers to build on. "Unlike central Melbourne, these suburbs don't have brownfield sites – disused docklands or railyards that can be home to high-rise residential towers. Unlike inner-city Fitzroy, Brunswick or Footscray, they have few warehouses or workshops that can be redeveloped into medium-density apartment blocks. And unlike the city's outer-urban growth areas, no greenfield sites are available to be transformed into housing estates."

The three YIMBY groups in Canberra, Melbourne and Sydney have got together and formed what they call the "Abundant Housing Network Australia" and have put in a submission to the current Senate inquiry into the rental crisis (yes, yet another inquiry). They are calling for a "more permissive and faster planning system," which I think gets to the heart of the issue. Their broad-brush ideas to increase Australia's urban density include:

- moving from prescriptive and arbitrary rules to a more permissive, outcomes-based regulation of land use and development (in other words, making it work for people, not for council bureaucrats)

- broad zoning changes across large areas, rather than specific sites

- facilitating development in high amenity areas well served by public and active transport and social infrastructure

- removing parking space minimums from developments near railway stations

- investigating mechanisms for the efficient and equitable consolidation of urban blocks, particularly small lots in residential areas

- ensuring the broader community is consulted, rather than just those with time and resources.

The fifth of those points would make a big difference, but there's no easy way to consolidate urban blocks to create what Peter Mares calls brownfield development sites.

In fact, let's face it, significantly increasing the density of housing within 10 to 30 kilometres of Australia's CBDs – which is what is required – is going to be difficult, if not impossible. A lot of the houses within 10 kilometres are Victorian or Edwardian terraces and villas and can't be pulled down for heritage reasons, and the "efficient and equitable consolidation of urban blocks," as the YIMBYs put it, is a lot easier said than done. People sell their houses at different times, and no government is going to compulsorily acquire them to suit the timing of a developer.

On top of that, the cartel of developers is holding back supply. Prosper Australia recently did a big study of Master Planned Communities (what used to be called housing estates) and found that after an average of 9.5 years of production time, developers still held 76.2 per cent of their land banks vacant. Instead of prices falling because of this potential supply, the average land price inflation was 5.5 per cent annually. By contrast, wage growth ran at only 2.4 per cent.

Says Prosper Australia: "If supply can be curtailed in this way, we suggest it shows that property markets are inherently monopolistic, rather than competitive, unlike markets for goods and services. Property is an asset: land banks are patiently managed and development projects are timed to maximise overall returns."

So as part of any housing affordability strategy, governments need to recognise the monopoly characteristics of the property market and get the Australian Competition and Consumer Commission (ACCC) involved. At the very least the ACCC should treat land development as it would any cartel and keep an eye on what's happening. At the moment there is a complete absence of government oversight.

One concrete way to deal with this would be to use taxes to increase the cost of holding land. At the moment it's obviously worthwhile for developers to pay the holding cost to boost their eventual sale price; the balance of that equation needs to tip the other way.

In any case, new housing estates – I mean Master Planned Communities, such as Jordan Springs near Penrith in New South Wales, 60 kilometres from Sydney's CBD – have very limited infrastructure. It's an hour's drive to Sydney on the freeway and an hour and a half on the train, and the nearest train station is between 5 and 10 kilometres away.

The only way to significantly increase the supply of "well-located" housing must be trains – fast ones, coupled with ACCC involvement in the housing development business.

I'm not talking about Japanese and Chinese-style "bullet trains," or the ones that might end up being built by the High Speed Rail Authority set up by the Albanese government in June 2023, but simply the sort of trains that ply the European countryside at 150 to 200 kilometres an hour.

For example, a new housing estate has been established on farmland at a place called Armstrong Creek, south of Geelong, about 100 kilometres from Melbourne's CBD. There's a railway station not far – at Marshall – and including the drive to the station, the train journey to Melbourne takes two hours. That's simply not viable for commuting, except to Geelong. The trip to Melbourne needs to take less than an hour, and if it did, a lot more people could live there and developers would build more houses there.

At the moment the viable commuting distance in Australia is no more than 50 kilometres, because the trains are slow and traffic is a nightmare, even on expensive toll roads. That can involve a commute of an hour and a half. The fact that most people want to crowd into that fifty-kilometre radius, and that it consists of mostly single dwellings on large blocks of land, is the fundamental cause of Australia's unaffordable housing.

Unless there a big and unlikely increase in the density of housing within 50 kilometres of the CBD, the commuting radius needs to extend to 100 to

200 kilometres. To make that happen, commuter trains need to travel 150 kilometres an hour, and preferably 200 kilometres per hour, so there can be a few stops while keeping the travel time to an hour.

To be a housing affordability solution, high-speed rail needs to radiate inland from the CBD, as well as up and down the coast. Specifically, commuters need to be able to live in Bathurst, 200 kilometres from the Sydney CBD and currently a four-hour train journey, and get to work in the city within an hour. Or Bendigo, 150 kilometres from Melbourne. Or Toowoomba, 125 kilometres from Brisbane, which currently takes two hours on the train.

What's needed is decentralisation of housing but not necessarily of employment, and that requires fast, efficient commuting trains that allow dormitory suburbs to be developed further from the CBD. That would dramatically increase the supply of "well-located" land as the government's housing policy describes it, without pushing against the natural barriers against medium-density housing closer to the city. In a way, the effort to squeeze more housing into a 50-kilometre radius from the CBD is really just an effort to avoid the cost of infrastructure. The trouble is, it won't work. All the talk about a lot more medium-density housing is just that – talk. It will never actually happen. What's needed is transport infrastructure.

There has been talk of fast trains in Australia for about forty years, but the discussion has always been about fast train travel between capital cities to replace air travel, not within the cities, to extend them. And even on that subject, Australia has been left standing at the platform. There are now about 60,000 kilometres of high-speed rail in the world, an increase of 35 per cent in just three years. There are over 44,000 kilometres of lines in the Asia-Pacific, mainly China and Japan, almost 12,000 in Europe and 1500 in the Middle East. And there's a lot more coming: those currently under construction will increase the length of the world's high-speed rail network by another 33 per cent.

None of them are or will be in Australia. Most other countries have been building railways for a century, starting with subways in the cities and then fast trains between them and between towns and suburbs, but Australia has stuck with cars and planes. The result is expensive housing.

Transport infrastructure in Australia is controlled by the airlines and the toll-road operators, but no one rich and powerful is pushing trains, and the projects that are put up are either too ambitious, not ambitious enough or ambitious in the wrong way. It's either a plan for a vastly expensive inter-capital city high-speed rail that never gets built, or Victoria's suburban rail loop, which will encircle Melbourne through the existing suburbs about 20 to 25 kilometres from the CBD at a cost of about $200 billion, if it ever gets built. Neither of those rail projects would open up new commuting suburbs and increase the supply of housing.

A serious and realistic effort to deal with housing affordability in Australia must involve a very big investment in trains designed to at least double, pref-erably triple, the commutable distance from the capital cities and industrial inner suburbs where people work. Yes, it would be expensive, and would involve the federal government paying for state government infrastructure, and issuing debt to do it, but every other solution looks too hard, no mat-ter what the cost.

Reducing demand by restricting negative gearing and increasing capital gains tax should happen, but probably won't. Linking immigration to hous-ing approvals? Also should happen, but unlikely. Increasing the supply of medium density in existing suburbs through better zoning and planning is more likely, but is still more talk than action, and will take more than a $15,000 bounty per approval capped at $3 billion.

Unless interest rates go high enough to cause a recession, or there's an unlikely crackdown on bank lending practices, Australia's housing afforda-bility problem can only realistically be solved with a national consensus that there is a problem, a clear statement about what needs to be achieved, and then trains, fast ones, lots of them, radiating from the CBDs.

The insidious damage of unaffordable housing has a political cause and a political solution, but its victims simply don't have enough political clout to make it happen. They are mainly the people born after the mid-1980s, who either can't enjoy the freedom and security that owning a place to live in can provide, or, if they do manage it, have no money left for anything else and no time for their kids because they have to work full-time, often in two jobs. But there's not enough of them to move the political dial.

It's not just that renters are in the minority – some minorities have real power – but that the nation's attitude to housing is deeply ambivalent and well hidden. There has been, and still is, a public dialogue about the problem of housing affordability and plenty of sympathy expressed for the disenfranchised, but the majority who own a house are quietly happy with their high prices, and at the same time economists and businesspeople approve of the economic "wealth effect." Also, the minority who don't own a house still talk about the property ladder and the need to get on it. The idea of housing as the main, if not the only, form of real wealth creation for ordinary people is deeply embedded in the national psyche. Superannuation is starting to rival it but is still a long way behind.

That means doing something about it requires true political leadership – that is, doing something right that's unpopular. Study after study on the subject has concluded that the high price of housing is leading to dangerous inequality and distorting the economy and society, yet political leaders have never tackled it effectively, for obvious reasons.

The fact that one of the three least populated countries on Earth contains the world's second-most expensive housing is a national calamity, and a stunning failure of public policy. For decades, political leaders have paid lip service to housing affordability while doing nothing about it that would bring prices down. In fact, most of the big political decisions have done the opposite.

For example, the capital gains tax discount in 1999 was designed by business leaders to encourage investing in their businesses, but it only led to a surge in investment in housing. Since then, there have been official inquiries and taskforces into housing affordability in 2003, 2004, 2008, 2009, 2012, 2013, 2014, 2015, 2016, 2018 and 2022. Throughout all this time, house prices kept rising, except when APRA cracked down on bank lending to investors in 2017, and when the Reserve Bank increased interest rates in 2022. Policy has been nowhere, done nothing.

When the ALP adopted its policy to modify negative gearing in 2016, and there was an opportunity for the political class to come together and actually achieve something, it was turned into another occasion for rivalry, and was later excluded from the terms of reference of yet another inquiry. Transport infrastructure decisions have usually favoured road, usually toll roads, not fast rail, and all the work on the latter has focused on the pie-in-the-sky of inter-capital city trains rather than anything designed to increase the supply of housing.

And perhaps most important of all, decisions about the level of immigration have been driven by the needs of business, with little thought to housing the new arrivals or to the impact on house prices.

So the bottom line is that Australian capital-city housing is too expensive compared to incomes for a healthy society, and that needs to change. Merely bringing the rate of increase in house prices back to the rate of growth in incomes isn't enough – that ratio needs to come down so it isn't a stretch to buy a place to live. To achieve this will require active, and serious, government intervention. It won't be enough simply to restore the amount of housing construction to what it was before the pandemic, as the federal government is now aspiring to do.

We don't need another inquiry or a royal commission; there's a room full of inquiries, reports and submissions. We just need a taskforce drawn from Treasury and the housing department to go through the work that's been done already and come up with a policy that has a clear aim and is likely to work. That would be a good start.

SOURCES

7   "zoning restrictions raised the average price of detached houses": Ross Kendall and Peter Tulip, *The Effect of Zoning on House Prices*, Research Discussion Paper 2018–03, Reserve Bank of Australia, 2018.

16   "a national survey found": Animal Medicines Australia, *Pets in Australia: A national survey of pets and people*, 16 November 2022.

17   "when housing affordability becomes a national issue": Committee for Economic Development in Australia, *Housing Australia*, August 2017, p. 9.

19–20 "It is a matter of history": W.E.H. Stanner, "After the Dreaming", The Boyer Lectures, 1968.

22   "To put that 1889 peak in perspective": Nigel Stapledon, *A History of Housing Prices in Australia, 1880–2010*, School of Economics Discussion Paper, The University of New South Wales Australian School of Business, September 2010.

26   79 per cent above the 1942 level: Stapledon, *A History of Housing Prices*.

27   "We consider": Leo Patrick Devereaux O'Connor, *Commonwealth Housing Commission final report*, 1944.

28   "Ryan and Willmott Phillips' contributions": Patrick Troy, *Accommodating Australians: Commonwealth involvement in housing*, Federation Press, 2012.

31   "home owners were seen": Patrick Troy, *The Rise and Fall of Public Housing in Australia*, conference paper, ANU Research Publications.

32   "One consequence of this": Troy, *Accommodating Australians*.

33   "The process of changing: Troy, *Accommodating Australians*.

38   "The most radical": Paul Collits, "Regional policy in post-war Australia: Much ado about nothing?", Productivity Commission, www.pc.gov.au/__data/assets/pdf_file/0004/218038/subdr040-transitioning-regions-attachment2.pdf.

43   "primer on zoning and its effects": Productivity Commission, *Victoria's Commercial Land Use Zoning*, Productivity Reform Case Study, July 2020.

46   "The document that will be most relevant": Tony Richards, "How to solve Australia's housing crisis", *Australian Financial Review*, May 2023.

61   "It's hard to think": Eslake, "Doling out cash to first home buyers hasn't made more of us home owners", *The Sydney Morning Herald*, 15 March 2011.

62   "served simply": Eslake, "Doling out cash".

79   between the 2011 and 2021 censuses: Peter Mares, "Flawed foundations," *Inside Story*, 8 September 2023.

81   "If supply": Prosper Australia, *Staged Released: Peering behind the land supply curtain*, July 2022.

Bill Shorten

Micheline Lee's essay *Lifeboat* is beautiful. It felt like truth and it resonated. In life we occasionally have light-bulb moments. Micheline's essay linked my gut subconscious understanding of life with a disability with my intellectual understanding of life with a disability. It is somehow both flattering and disconcerting that my analogy for the plight of the National Disability Insurance Scheme (NDIS), as "the only lifeboat in the ocean" for people with disability, was used as a cornerstone of this important essay.

Micheline's essay is an intensely personal lens on the individuality of people when we speak or do anything about disability. Her piece gives the reader a first-hand window onto the NDIS and the journey for access to equality in the world as a whole.

In my opinion, there has never been a better time in our nation's history than now to talk about the human rights of people with disability. In politics, to achieve real change, timing is everything. We have just had the Royal Commission into Violence, Abuse, Neglect and Exploitation of People with Disability, which Labor first called for in May 2017, hand down its final report, including 222 recommendations for change. And the NDIS Review, which I established soon after Labor came to government in 2022, will also deliver its recommendations.

The final report of the Disability Royal Commission challenges us to create a more inclusive Australia where individuals live with dignity, equality and respect, and can fulfil their potential. Volume four of the final report pertains to human rights. It recommends an "overhaul of Australia's legislative policy and governance structures to protect the right of people with disability."

We should seize the day for a horizon project across Australian society to ensure people with disability are able to be included, whether this be going to the school of their choice, making and meeting friends, studying, working, living or enjoying themselves and moving around with the form of mobility that works best for them.

We can make a national decision to journey to the horizon of the most inclusive nation in the world.

The Albanese government has set up a taskforce to respond to the 222 recommendations, led by the very capable Amanda Rishworth, Minister for Social Services, who will provide a progress update early next year. I am very mindful of the Convention on the Rights of Persons with Disabilities being used to underpin our efforts. While the NDIS Review is independent, I also have no doubt the human rights of people with disability will wash through every aspect of the important final report.

Micheline visits the scheme as a participant, family member, mother, friend, lawyer and formidable intellect. She navigates the world bringing these various perspectives, but also from a deeply personal, unique place. Most importantly, her essay reminds those of us with the privilege of power and the capacity to make change, whether basic or transformational, that we cannot make any meaningful impact without people with disability as co-design partners.

When I first became involved with the disability sector in 2007 in the Rudd government, "Nothing about us without us" was the anthem of people with disability in their campaign for the fair go. Since 2007, I have seen and been part of the campaign for a scheme that would provide universal and lifelong support for people who are significantly and permanently disabled. Alongside every person with a disability and their families and advocates, we won the right to establish the NDIS. In 2013 the dream became a reality for hundreds of thousands of Australians with disability.

The scheme was legislated by Labor and then piloted and rolled out by successive Coalition governments. From Opposition, nothing frustrated me more than watching the scheme being run down over nine years. On a daily basis I heard about the life-changing, positive changes the NDIS had brought for many, but also horror stories of how, for too many participants and families, navigating the NDIS was an inconsistent, opaque, dehumanising "second full-time job."

While I didn't know Micheline's friend Frida, I believe the shocking, avoidable death of South Australian woman Ann Marie Smith in 2020 taught a similar lesson. Ann Marie's passing was a pivotal moment in the collective realisation that the NDIS was not doing what it was supposed to; people were not being kept safe from harm.

After my election loss as Labor leader to Scott Morrison, I understood that the universe does not grant reruns. But the universe has a funny way of surprising. With every precious minute in the job as NDIS minister, I do feel I've been given a remarkable second chance to return to fix up the scheme I helped create.

On first being given the shadow NDIS ministry after the 2019 election and then seeking the important role of NDIS minister in the Albanese Labor government in 2022, I was given the chance to serve where I know I can repay the gift of faith and goodwill and lessons from Australians with disability. Now that I am in charge of the scheme, I have a bird's-eye view of how the "choice and control" the NDIS was supposed to offer was being micromanaged by governments and bureaucracies which clearly did not think people with disability could make decisions about their own lives.

After ten years, the NDIS has the momentum to return to its original purpose, to be here to stay, to become "politician-proof." That's why *Lifeboat* hits a raw nerve, because it pinpoints the pressure the scheme has been under since its creation. Despite diabolical management, the scheme has remained a fundamental structure in Australia's safety net ecosystem. As Micheline notes, there are now more than 600,000 Australians with disability who are NDIS participants, but they are part of almost 4.5 million people with disability across the nation.

Micheline writes almost hesitantly about the collective role of governments to provide support, choice and accessibility, as though the premise is built on a house of cards. I understand that fear, but I am with her all the way to help people with disability and the people who love them.

We must remember that the NDIS was only intended to be one part of a broader disability support ecosystem. But that ecosystem isn't working as intended. It's on all of us to commit to greater investment and effort to create inclusion: schools, transport, early childhood, community activities, advocacy, building regulations, community mental health by all levels of governments and the private sector. And there must be a discussion with states and territories about all of us lifting our outcomes in disability support. There is momentum for a better and more consistent deal. The parts of the ecosystem are being brought together.

The Disability Royal Commission was the culmination of four and half years of broad consultation. The 222 recommendations will be carefully considered; the report will not sit on a shelf collecting dust. I acknowledge that not every recommendation is automatically accepted; rather, the sum of the work is critical. Nor will the NDIS Review report sit on a shelf after it is handed to the Disability Reform Ministerial Council.

Too much of the NDIS's ten-year history was left to be written by Coalition governments which, in my opinion, did not understand the human rights foundation of the world-first scheme. Successive governments ran down the National Disability Insurance Agency by imposing unreasonable staffing caps, resulting in a lack of capacity and a lack of capability. How could 4500 staff who serviced

150,000 participants at the start of the scheme be expected to give the same level of attention to the 660,000 Australians who now access the scheme?

Participants have been faced with the horrible situation of long delays in their package being approved and having to explain their needs to people who lacked knowledge about their disability or disease. We're changing that, with the largest investment ever made in the NDIA. That funding means recruiting more staff and ensuring better training and systems so that the agency is fit for purpose.

We're committed to co-designing policies with people with disability and making sure those with lived experience have a seat at the table where decisions are made. We have already made significant changes to the membership of the NDIA board and the agency's senior management.

We're recognising that one size does not fit all and we're building flexibility into the way services are delivered, especially in remote and Indigenous communities.

And we are stopping the fraud and rorting that has seen money that was meant for participants line the pockets of crooks and dodgy providers that taint the reputation of many hardworking and decent providers. No more. That ends. We are locking the back door of the scheme that Coalition government left wide open.

I don't dismiss any of the criticisms of the NDIS, nor do I think I can wave a magic wand and make it instantly perfect. But I can promise you that I am doing everything in my power to return the NDIS to its original intent. It is a life-changing scheme for thousands of Australians with disability and I want to make sure that is the reality for every person who is eligible and accesses the NDIS.

The underlying mission is to make the NDIS sustainable for generations to come of Australians with disability. To do that, we have to listen to current NDIS participants about where it has gone off the rails. Micheline's essay gives us a chair's-eye view. It perfectly encapsulates the human experience of disability. It uplifts because it reminds the reader impairment is a fact of life, not the problem. The problem is a lack of money and power and an inability to see past one attribute of another human. I thank her for sharing what is a deeply personal account.

Micheline mentions the great Professor Bruce Bonyhady AM a number of times in Lifeboat. Professor Bonyhady is co-chair of the NDIS Review, with esteemed former public servant and policymaker Lisa Paul AO PSM.

Bruce Bonyhady recently quoted the seventeenth-century English writer John Donne's potent meditation, "No man is an island," on the way all parts of society have the potential to intersect with the lives of people with disability. How we are all part of the "village" that supports and enriches our sense of community. In Donne's famous meditation, the poet reminds us that each of us plays a role "because I am involved in mankind."

We are all part of the rich tapestry of life. Better to do it together than alone.

> No man is an island,
> Entire of itself,
> Every man is a piece of the continent,
> A part of the main.
> If a clod be washed away by the sea,
> Europe is the less.
> As well as if a promontory were.
> As well as if a manor of thy friend's
> Or of thine own were:
> Any man's death diminishes me,
> Because I am involved in mankind,
> And therefore never send to know for whom the bell tolls;
> It tolls for thee.

Bill Shorten

Monique Ryan

One in six Australians live with disability. That's 4.4 million people. To support them, ten years ago the Gillard Labor government established the National Disability Insurance Scheme. The NDIS has been life-changing for many Australians. For many, the supports it has provided have been essential to living an included life within our society – possibly for the first time – but the ten-year mark for this scheme coincides with a time of uncertainty and concern regarding increasing participant numbers and rapidly escalating cost. Micheline Lee's Quarterly Essay *Lifeboat* is therefore perfectly timed, landing as it does at the same time as the report of the Royal Commission into Violence, Abuse, Neglect and Exploitation of People with Disability – all twelve volumes and 6788 pages of it – and the impending final report of the independent review commissioned by the NDIS minister, Bill Shorten, in October 2022.

The Australian Labor Party prides itself on Medicare, its universal healthcare scheme, established by the Whitlam government in 1975. The fundamental principles of Medibank/Medicare were equity, efficiency, simplicity and fairness in provision of a universal insurance scheme for healthcare provided under the shared auspices of the Commonwealth and the states and territories. The NDIS has never quite reached for or achieved those lofty ideals, but it has become a major part of our government's social welfare system.

The NDIS was designed to give disabled individuals "reasonable and necessary" supports, over which they have choice and control as to how they want to live their life, and over who delivers the supports required to help them achieve this. Many current issues with the NDIS relate to its structure. It was established as an insurance scheme in the expectation that early investment in the capacity of those with significant disability would decrease the cost of their future care. The scheme was aimed primarily at Australians with permanent and significant deficits – so-called "Tier 3" individuals – who would be given personalised individual support packages. Similar packages would be provided to those with less severe disability where it was predicted that early intervention would significantly lessen their future support needs. Approximately 475,000 such cases were anticipated, and it was expected that community-based disability services – including education, health and vocational training – would support the remaining 3.8 million Australians with lesser disability ("Tier 2" individuals). Those in Tier 2 would continue to receive mainstream health, education and employment support via mainstream (generally state-based) services. The NDIS was never intended to cater for all Australians with a disability, or even for all of those with severe deficits: those over sixty-five were carved out, unless they entered the scheme before that age.

The reality of the NDIS as it stands now is very different. Almost from inception, the NDIS has become the back-up and default service for most children and adults with developmental disorders, delays and disabilities, as other disability supports and programs – particularly those funded by state and territory governments – have been defunded or removed. Vacation of the space previously filled by community-based block-funded services has left a void for those with milder developmental delay and physical deficits. Massive inequity has arisen; those on the scheme receive much more support than non-participants. The Melbourne Disability Service has reported that 90 per cent of people without NDIS funding are unable to access the supports they need. This renders current clients desperate to retain NDIS funding, and leaves others fighting to become eligible. Those with lower support needs have had to apply for NDIS funding when they might otherwise have accessed other programs, and paediatricians (like me) have been quicker to diagnose autism when that's the quickest and easiest way to ensure that children can receive early intervention for their developmental delay. When all you have is a hammer, everything starts looking a lot like a nail. However, this has led to a situation where 11 per cent of Australian five- to seven-year-old boys and 5 per cent of five- to seven-year-old girls are NDIS participants. This is simply unsustainable. It demands change.

The NDIS was established as a classic market-based system; the thought was that participants would drive and shape the market – that with control over their own plans they would select the best providers, rewarding excellence with patronage and driving competition for their services. The Productivity Commission assumed that supply would be generated in response to increased demand for providers, but the reality is that there remain shortages of many allied health disciplines and other providers in the disability sector. Disability care is not akin to fast-food delivery; you can't just call in a gig workforce of Uber drivers, although services such as Mabel have sprung up to attempt to fill the gap for lower-qualified workers able to provide less complex services. In many cases, the thin – and complex – market means that appropriately skilled providers often can't be found or accessed. For instance, disturbingly, people with psychosocial disability in the Far West region of New South Wales use only 11 per cent of their plans. The market fails where participants need more specialised supports, which come at higher costs, and in areas where there are poor economies of scale. The federal and state governments have not monitored disability services to ensure that there's back-up in regional or rural settings, that the services billed are actually provided, and that vulnerable participants are receiving not just services but also holistic care. There are no means by which people with disabilities can compare and rank service providers; and in any case their needs are individual and often complex. It can take a participant months to get to know and trust a carer; it's not as simple as comparing a pair on a website and swiping right. Because of the shortages of providers, those in the market have been able to raise their prices to the maximum permitted by the scheme, to levels above those supported by other services – TAC, Veterans' Affairs, Aged Care – so that individuals in those other schemes struggle to compete.

It's not all clover for the providers. The policy and compliance framework can be challenging, screening processes for workers slow, and cashflow an issue when clients neglect to pay accounts or run out of funds. Not-for-profits caring for high-needs and complex participants have found it difficult to compete for staff and to provide their services competitively. Cost-shifting between the federal and state governments does not help. In August 2023, the Victorian government tried to cut funding for specialist visiting teachers working with disabled children in schools, backflipping only in the face of sustained outrage from parents, teachers and disability advocacy groups. During the pandemic, issues with NDIS-funded planners left hospitalised scheme participants ready for discharge waiting for an average of 118 days – ready to go home but waiting on funding packages and accommodation.

There are clearly significant inequities in how the NDIS is operating. NDIS participants are overwhelmingly young and male. Only 37 per cent of NDIS participants are women. This reflects the higher incidence of autism and related conditions in males, but it also reflects selection bias within the scheme; 49 per cent of people with disability aged under sixty-five years are female. Plan utilisation is higher for those in metropolitan than in regional and remote areas. Many participants describe inconsistencies in the size of support packages provided to people with the same disability or level of need. The quality of advocacy by planners and parents has mattered, disadvantaging those whose advocates argue less eloquently, those with less familiarity with bureaucracy, and those from culturally and linguistically diverse backgrounds. Lower levels of plan utilisation among Indigenous people with disabilities reflect difficulties with providing evidence of disability and an absence of whole-of-life case management in the NDIS for those who are dealing not only with disability but also with other social challenges such as homelessness and poverty.

Cost has been a perennial concern. The NDIS is a demand-driven scheme with no limits on spending. As of June 2023, the scheme has more than 610,000 participants, with numbers projected to increase to over a million by 2032. Fraud is an issue, as with all government systems, but the extent and prevalence of system abuse is unclear. Attempts to rein spending in under the Morrison government led to cost-cutting, and a 400 per cent increase in disputes over packages. We all know that the disability dollar is not unlimited. The NDIS is expected to cost $50 billion annually by 2024/25 – more than the annual budget for Medicare, or even defence, nuclear submarines notwithstanding. That figure, however, fails to take into account the original assumption of the scheme: that it would generate revenue and productivity by facilitating employment and engagement of people with disabilities, and by freeing up carers to return to the workforce. While employment of disabled people has not increased significantly in the past ten years, there is good evidence that the multiplier effect of the NDIS is significant – that every dollar spent generates an economic contribution of $2.25. It's a service, not an expense.

As a paediatric neurologist, I interacted with the NDIS through the annual completion of support letters, which very often had to be rewritten as I'd not used the right key words to trigger maximal package size. I had to undertake yearly redocumentation of the permanence of genetic conditions. I had to do my best to convince assessors that NDIS funding was just as justified for individuals with life-long, progressive disorders as for those with conditions more likely to respond to intervention. I had to apologise to parents for documents emphasising their children's deficits, in the hope of attracting more support, rather than highlighting their engagement with therapy and their capacity for achievement.

As a member of parliament, I hear often from NDIS participants and their carers about their frustration and anger with the system. From the mother of a brain-injured adult in Supported Independent Living, worried about the potential for his 24-hour nursing care to be revoked. From the sisters of a disabled adult concerned with the increasing cost of his residential placement. From the guardians of a thirteen-year-old with autism and fetal alcohol spectrum disorder, whose excellent Special Developmental School struggles to manage her behavioural outbursts and who can't access inpatient psychiatric care where her medications can be safely adjusted. From consumers outraged that the NDIS is paying large amounts for behavioural therapy assessments of dubious value. From participants and parents unable to find affordable, accessible psychologists, psychiatrists, dieticians, speech pathologists or occupational therapists. Those engaged with the scheme were outraged by the comment of the previous CEO of the National Disability Insurance Agency, Martin Hoffman, that the NDIS "operates on the presumption that all people with disability have the capacity to make decisions and exercise choice and control." That comment was made at a Royal Commission hearing into the death of Ann Marie Smith, a 54-year-old woman with cerebral palsy who died from septic shock, organ failure and malnutrition at the hands of an NDIS provider. It reflected a refusal to accept that the ability to exercise choice and control is often compromised in persons with a disability. Of course it is – how could it be otherwise? The NDIS's remit must not only ensure support to help people exercise independence but also include a duty of care for those unable to do so.

As a member of the Australian Parliament's Joint Standing Committee on the NDIS, I've had the honour of hearing from many providers and participants about their experience of the system. Some of those testimonials were really hard to hear; they were raw, confronting, sometimes heartbreaking. Our NDIS has the potential to be world-leading, but it has become adversarial. Participants are expected to justify why their static or progressive medical conditions are not improving. They're forced to undergo annual assessments which engender uncertainty and anxiety, when there is often no good reason for such frequent reviews. They've had to take on review processes and the Administrative Appeals Tribunal without support or representation. We have forced disabled Australians – and their parents, partners and carers – to battle a system in which transparency and generosity have been sacrificed to red tape and mean-spirited bureaucracy.

So the question remains: how do we best support those needing help? We should, can and must do better than we have done to date with this life-changing scheme. Shorten sees the NDIS as "the only lifeboat in the ocean." Bruce Bonyhady, the original chair of the National Disability Insurance Agency, has described it as an "oasis in the desert." Rather than the individual supports provided by the NDIS, we have to offer a dual system, including both defined packages for those with more significant needs, and community-based programs for infants and young children with developmental delay, children with mild autism and neurodivergence, and adults with milder deficits for whom group therapy will not only result in better use of resources but might also promote inclusion. This model will be better aligned with the original NDIS design. It will also be more cost-effective. Politicians love a metaphor; I'll offer an alternative. No man is an island, or an oasis, and no man should need a lifeboat. The NDIS should be a trampoline; a place for soft landings with strong external supports and limits, but also a launch-ing pad for those able to take off. Around that trampoline should be the soft grass provided by support services which increase the range and nature of community and mainstream supports for people without severe disability, and which provide group therapy and services for all who are able to benefit from them. This model would need us to resile from the premise that all disabled people must self-manage their care, and that all should receive support individually. Some things are better done together – for efficiency, economy and enjoyment. The model would also mean that, as a society, we accept our responsibility to include and support all individuals, their variations and imperfections, and to create a context accepting of their varying capacities and needs.

Monique Ryan

Sam Drummond

Micheline Lee describes working as a lawyer and being rejected by a client as soon as he sees her. "He told the manager that he needed a lawyer who would look the part in court."

This is an all-too-common experience for disabled professionals. We've been told our whole lives that we should fit in, make ourselves useful: in Lee's words, "deny and overcome." Then, when we do, we find out there's a certain view of what a successful person looks like – and it isn't disabled.

Lee's experience with a client highlights the unspoken reality disabled people face every day. We hear so often that Australia is the land of the "fair go," but what does that actually mean? Does it mean that everyone should have the support they need to live a life they love? Or does it mean everyone gets treated the same, even when that means unequal outcomes?

Lee is sceptical of the whole concept – and who can blame her? It is with this scepticism that she analyses the current state of the National Disability Insurance Scheme.

Perhaps the greatest strength and the greatest weakness of advocating for disability rights is that everyone says they support them, from shelf stackers at the supermarket to politicians. Even in today's polarised environment, it's only someone right on the outer fringes who would say "I'm against disability rights" out loud.

But when it comes to the crunch, will they willingly reach up to the top shelf to help us get an item? Will they support our right to lead as meaningful a life as theirs? The reality is that people with disability can't count on the answer to this question being yes. We strive for independence, but too often it is labelled as stubbornness.

It was with this doubt in our minds that we realised our humanity wasn't enough to get the NDIS over the line. In our society, a life is not worth as much as others until there is economic output. And so we embraced an economic model.

Lee describes sector elder Bruce Bonyhady's light-bulb moment talking to then deputy prime minister Brian Howe, who advised him to frame disability policy as risk insurance and investment rather than welfare. The spectre of Bonyhady looms large over Lee's essay, like the Architect from the Matrix, who creates a system that keeps the machines powered and the humans at bay through the construct of choice. Lee invites us to sit with Bonyhady's description of the choice faced by the scheme's creators. "Insurance appeals to people's self-interest in a way that human rights don't," he said. "Some people see human rights as something that a minority goes on about too loudly and so an emphasis on human rights might have risked rejection of the NDIS."

Without Bonyhady, we may not have the NDIS at all. He worked with thousands of other disability activists to advocate tirelessly for this life-changing policy. The choice they faced was critical to its sustainability – tell the story of how every human is equal or sell the scheme as one of economic efficiency.

It took us decades of thinking about disability in new ways to get to the NDIS. We passed the word from person to person, any way we could, that the disadvantages experienced by people with disability are the barriers put up by society – a lack of ramps, inaccessible toilets, strobe lighting, a lack of plain-language information.

Julia Gillard called the NDIS "the greatest change to Australian social policy in a generation." Yet to sell the social change to our neighbours, it was framed as an economic reform. As suggested by Brian Howe, it was called an insurance scheme.

Perhaps the existential problem the NDIS faces goes to the heart of insurance as a concept. You insure yourself against something bad happening – a crash on a road, a fire in your house, an unfortunate mishap with your pet labradoodle. Nobody said it better than the late Stella Young: "We have been lied to about disability. We've been sold the lie that disability is a bad thing. Capital B, capital T. It's a bad thing." You get insurance so a bad thing doesn't happen.

People without disabilities bought the NDIS because they didn't want the bad thing to happen to them. People with disabilities knew this. We've always known the risk that a fair go doesn't include actual equality. This was the trade-off to lifting our standard of living towards that of the wider population.

Fast-forward to now and we are seeing the results of a human rights scheme built on sandy foundations that sidelined human rights. The economic imperative of the scheme's structure has inevitably seen a retreat towards disability as a medical diagnosis – away from the social model of disability that informed its creation. It is a scheme we should be grateful for as a charitable act by the taxpayer.

I've heard the suggestion that the I in NDIS should be changed to Investment. In my opinion, that too falls into the trap of seeing a person as a dollar figure. We are not people but consumers, left to the whims of providers. We are not contributors to a successful society but burdens on the taxpayer. Our independence is reduced once more to stubbornness.

The ultimate question that Lee's essay asks is this: what is the future of the scheme?

It also asks: Is disability a normal part of what it means to be human? Is it something our society can embrace not for its economic opportunity (although Lee points out that the numbers do stack up) but for the fact that we are your friends, children, parents and neighbours?

While putting people with disability at the centre of decision-making is key – and is in fact required by international law – the burden of the answer must fall to people without disability. Compare Lee's legal client to the woman she encounters at the airport. An airport security staffer tells Lee she should have a support worker with her to lift her bag onto the security conveyor belt. This situation clearly wouldn't have happened before the NDIS. The woman behind Lee mutters, "Unbelievable," and lifts the bag up.

The wider population can't be bystanders waiting for people with disabilities to do the heavy lifting. It's not on us to fix the holes that opened up because people without disabilities were assured the NDIS was in their self-interest. Yes, we need to fix the scheme. But human rights must be at the centre.

Lee writes that "it is through acceptance of our universal condition of vulnerability that the attitudes in our society which cause segregation are most likely to be changed." To be human is to be vulnerable.

"Disability was something I had to deny and overcome," Lee says. "This mindset influenced the way I tried to live right up until my twenties." This rings true for so many people with a disability. We have already been on the journey of accepting this. It's up to others to come on that journey too.

So, to those wanting to know how to fix the scheme: read Lee's essay and be like that woman at the airport. Shake your head and mutter, "Unbelievable," while lifting the NDIS to where it should be – with human rights at its heart.

Sam Drummond

Rhonda Galbally

Lifeboat is a comprehensive analysis and valuable critique of where we have got to with disability in Australia and where we might go. More than that, it is a beautifully written and very moving account of Lee's life as a disabled woman. Lee's status as a compelling writer was established with her wonderful novel *The Healing Party* and this essay applies her honed skill of drawing on her internal voice so that her inner ambiguities and struggles are revealed. This is a generously revealing approach – weaving together the personal and political – and Lee has done this with great skill in analysing the NDIS, warts and all.

Lee begins by outlining just a few of her struggles with Australia's lack of accessibility and inclusion. She wants to be polite and generous to people's well-intentioned efforts to be kind, but she reveals her inner rage at charitable attitudes, with its object the poor cripple and she on the receiving end.

On receiving a free bar of soap as a gift from a shop owner, she writes:

> I felt conflicted and embarrassed but didn't want to hurt his feelings.
> I approached and gave him a smile . . .
> "Aren't we just inspirational!" . . .
> "He was just being kind . . . he's better than most people," my sister added.
> "But it made you feel like a child, right?"

While being treated as brave, inspirational, vulnerable and needing protection might not sound too awful, it has led to awful treatment. Disabled people are segregated "for their own protection." Yet, as I found as a Disability Royal Commissioner, segregation enables violence, abuse, neglect and exploitation to abound unseen, invisible – out of sight and out of mind.

At the Disability Royal Commission we heard that the alternative is to make all systems in Australian society accessible and fully inclusive – starting with early childhood, so that disabled children can interact with non-disabled children in all aspects of schooling as one of the gang. It is familiarity that leads to acceptance that in turn enables attitudes to change. And Lee agrees that all systems – state, federal and local – need to fully include disabled people – health, housing, transport, education, employment, infrastructure.

Meanwhile, into our inaccessible, excluding Australia, the NDIS was launched, opening its doors in 2013 after an outstanding campaign called Every Australian Counts. There were huge hopes for the scheme, but it was never envisaged that it would have to take responsibility for the complete lack of universal access and inclusion. Its job was to enable people at an individual level to decide what they needed personally to participate fully in the social, cultural and economic life of Australia. The NDIS packages were only ever meant to be the personal bit of the equation. The external world also needed to be transformed so that disabled people could participate.

Nevertheless, the NDIS was a revolution, in that for the first time ever disabled people could decide what they needed and wanted and what personal support might assist them to get there. Lee describes valuing her independence and privacy, so she gets to choose how, when and where she gets support. She also tells of trying to persuade her friend Frida, who has a psychosocial disability, to take a package by describing how that could support her to get back to work.

Frida rejects the suggestion to go onto the NDIS. "I want a man," she says. Would, could or should a package have assisted Frida to go to places where she might find a man, or at least have a chance to make more friends that might lead to relationships? Frida did not have problems with physical access, but most places where we might meet people – disabled and non-disabled together – are completely inaccessible physically and socially forbidding to many people with disabilities, thereby excluding them.

Lee describes terrible cases of people trying to work their way through far too complex processes; dealing with inconsistent, unfair and irrational decisions; and trying endlessly to find what they need in undeveloped, thin markets. Do I detect, though, a slight hint of harking back to the old days when the states provided disability services with block funding, or am I being oversensitive? I regard the pre-NDIS service sector with horror: it was a time when disabled people had no choice or control – absolutely no say over what, how, who, when and if they would receive services, and certainly no say over the design of the specialist, mostly segregated services. And these segregated services were just as riddled with violence, abuse, neglect and exploitation, but with the addition that hardly anyone received support in the first place.

While Lee focuses on the market for disability specialist services, there needs to be attention given to the completely undeveloped "market" for mainstream services and systems. This means, for example, that people need a disability support worker to drive them around because public transport is not accessible. Or an occupational therapist to help them negotiate a place in what should be an inclusive and welcoming setting, such as a junior sports group, or a speech therapist to coach them in subjects at school.

If I, as a disabled woman, decide that I'd rather learn computing or reading or numeracy or photography or art with non-disabled people, the venue is likely to be inaccessible and the teacher is also likely to be unwilling and unable to teach me if I am non-verbal, intellectually disabled, have high support needs or diverse behaviours.

When the mainstream is inaccessible, it is far easier to default to a segregated special school, sheltered workshop, day program and group house, where I live, learn, work and play with my own kind. This is, in effect, to be forced into a segregated life rather than for the outside world of community living, mainstream schools, open employment and recreation to accept and include and teach disabled children and adults. Is the NDIS inadvertently expanding segregation in areas such as group homes, day programs and sheltered employment? If so, this is a profound problem and certainly not a lifeboat for those living in those settings.

Alternatively, is the NDIS adhering sufficiently to the original design, to provide flexible personal budgets that encourage the non-disability specialist mainstream world to include disabled people?

Lee implies that expecting consumer demand to transform the mainstream world is unrealistic and I agree with her. Governments should be taking responsibility for making all systems accessible and inclusive, not just because it is a requirement of their commitment to the human rights of persons with disabilities but also because this would take financial pressure off the NDIS.

The NDIS was never expected or funded to deliver an accessible and inclusive world. But in the face of an inaccessible community, fighting to get a package is the only game in town and the packages must be large enough to compensate for lack of access and inclusion.

The reality for the sustainability of the NDIS is that we need disabled people to be able to lead lives out in the world. What is needed is the combination of NDIS support packages that assist people to join the wider community and governments at all levels, ensuring we have accessible and inclusive systems and settings that enable this. It is this combination which provides the lifeboat referred to by Lee in the title of her essay.

At the heart of Lee's multilayered analysis of the NDIS, she grapples with the concept of individual/personal budgets. Personal self-directed budgets are a separate issue from market models or the consumer role. Lee herself is a self-managed participant and she outlines some of those choices that she makes – some of which work out and some don't, but all are hers to make.

In being concerned that self-directed budgets with choice at their heart might lead to a neoliberal consumerist approach, Lee quotes Mark Considine, who seems to be suggesting that we might consider giving up choice for voice. This made my blood pressure go up very high. Voice without choice means no choice about when, how, who and what for our daily lives – no choice about whom you live with, who supports you, what you eat, when. No choice to be able to leave your segregated setting and live your life in the community. Voice would be meaningless without choice. I'm sure that can't be what Considine would like to see, but I would guard the NDIS's choice and control aspiration to my last gasp and promote self-direction and flexible budgets as empowering, enabling the transition to mainstream life. At the same time, I recognise that the mainstream has a long way to go to ensure inclusion of disabled people.

Lee's essay is a call to arms to get the NDIS working much better. My hope, as a recent Disability Royal Commissioner, is that the NDIS, with its self-directed budgets enabling choice and control, will end up stimulating the demand by disabled people for an ordinary life in the mainstream. But this will only come to fruition if, as commissioners recommend, there is a commitment to the responsible phasing out of segregated models of housing, work and schooling. This would be properly spearheaded by governments at all levels agreeing to fully honour Australia's commitment to the treaty we were one of the first countries to sign: the Convention on the Rights of Persons with Disabilities.

Rhonda Galbally

Sam Bennett

I had not read Micheline Lee's work before but will be seeking it out in future. Her essay is a powerful and insightful combination of her internalised and deeply personal journey living with disability and a wider socio-historical account of evolving disability policy in Australia. Her essay lands us squarely in the present with a passionate critique of the issues she and other people with disability currently face with the National Disability Insurance Scheme.

Lee takes aim at the highly bureaucratic and disempowering NDIS planning process, the deficiencies and limitations she sees as inherent in the marketisation of disability support, and the many failings which have resulted from those with lived expertise being shut out of implementation.

The independent review of the NDIS will hand its report to government at the end of October. This is the latest review tasked with the daunting prospect of charting a course ahead that ensures the NDIS delivers on its objectives while restoring the fractured trust of participants and the wider public. The other focus of the review is sustainability; Micheline sees no evidence of sustainability issues, but this is clearly vexing Treasury and National Cabinet.

Reports of provider sharp practice, fraudulent behaviour, uncontrolled cost growth and violence and abuse directed at people with disability in NDIS-funded services make for a particularly turbulent context. There is a palpable feeling that these compounding events and heighted tensions are building towards another defining period for disability in Australia.

Yet there is an optimism in Lee's essay, stemming from the belief that mistakes can be corrected and there are strong foundations to build upon to further transform the attitudes that disadvantage people with disability in our society. Further, Lee's confidence that the inevitable human experience of eventual dependence and vulnerability will ultimately bind us together more strongly than our differences separate us is a profoundly positive point on which to end. Given the many examples she recounts of how far we have still to go, her optimism shimmers even more brightly.

Lee offers a broad perspective on the issues that must be tackled to fix the NDIS, but steers away from the specifics of what needs to change, which is only implied. One surprising aspect for me was the comparison of the NDIS with previous state and territory disability systems to illustrate problems with the current state of play. This applies specifically to the government's previous role as case manager and a provider of last resort, but also forms part of a broader critique of the government's withdrawal from direct service delivery and the folly of adopting a posture of "steer, not row."

The implication is that elements of the previous block-funded approach compare favourably, particularly the lack of reliance on markets to respond to low-volume/high-needs situations and the fact that participants were not previously weighed down by the label and sometimes burdensome reality of being seen as consumers. There is encouragement here for the NDIS Review to redress the balance, with reference to the government taking on more responsibility for commissioning and service delivery.

These are important debates and the analysis is thought-provoking. But when following this narrative to its possible conclusions, I start to get more than a little uncomfortable. The NDIS can be seen as part of a global evolution in disability policy towards self-directed funding as a pathway to greater independence, equity and inclusion. Lee's piece is eloquent on this and how far the NDIS has fallen short of its goals. The market looms large in the why. But if you look at the international comparisons, which Lee herself references, you sees that contemporary disability systems are all characterised, to a greater or lesser degree, by participant-directed support within some form of market-based model.

There are good reasons for these shifts in policy, driven as they were by the conviction of people with disability that directly controlling funding would lead to more of it being used on the things they need to live a full life and less on the things they don't.

The danger here is that old ways of thinking and working swept away by the NDIS reform find a foothold and a new language that supports their re-emergence in ways that those advocating change might not anticipate. Old habits die hard, particularly in government bureaucracies steeped in the persistent rituals of welfare.

Mine is not an argument for the status quo: the disability support market clearly needs better tilling and tending than it has been afforded, including in some of the areas Lee's essay highlights. But a word of caution is warranted regarding the risks in swinging too far back the other way, towards government service delivery.

Rather than winding back the clock, changes enacted from here should focus on what is needed to make the market more diverse and more accountable.

The absence of any clear vision articulated by governments regarding the shape of the disability market it wants to see is perplexing. That the NDIS embraces a market-based model does not mean governments should be agnostic to its development or that they should assume that consumer choice will on its own deliver desirable policy outcomes when it comes to equity and inclusion. Yet concerted forays into market shaping have been very limited to date, almost solely focused on the important issue of thin markets in regional and remote Australia.

Another focus for Lee is the miasma of bureaucracy that is the current NDIS planning process, which ties people with disability in knots and has embedded a fraught and adversarial negotiation around every item of support at the heart of the scheme.

Lee writes, "The plan is a big deal. If a support is not clearly covered by a plan or explicitly listed, then it won't be funded" and "the planning process is notoriously disempowering."

The reason for this is that NDIS planning is not actually planning at all. It is an administratively complex process of resource allocation that itemises a list of permissible expenditure. It does so because the plan is currently the NDIS's primary cost-control mechanism, a task for which it has proved woefully ill-equipped.

Planning in the NDIS today involves more than 10,000 decisions a week, made using highly subjective "reasonable and necessary" criteria within increasingly short timeframes, as staff numbers have not kept pace with participant growth. The process invites conflict, dispute, inequity and inflationary pressure. And any scheme whose financial performance rests on the sum of thousands of decisions made by junior public servants working to vague instruction will always come unstuck in the end.

NDIS planning serves nobody well. This is not how individualised funding systems are supposed to work and conforms to no established principle of best practice. Which brings me to the final point that struck me reading Lee's critique – her perspective that the issues with the NDIS are primarily those of implementation. While it is undoubtedly the case that all manner of things could (and probably should) have been better implemented over the first ten years of the NDIS, the critical issues outlined with planning and markets are fundamentally ones of design.

Thankfully, you don't have to look too hard to get a sense of the better design choices available. The planning issues that Lee identifies could be fixed by adopting the common design features of other systems of self-directed support and personal budgets, such as in the UK. This would involve the separation of resource allocation from planning so that funding entitlements are transparently connected to a standardised process of assessment rather than the current line-by-line plan-build approach.

This would also breathe life into the prospect of real planning occurring in the NDIS for the first time. Participants under this model would be free to plan creatively and choose support from wherever they liked (for instance, their local disability organisation, which understands the community well), because planning does not have to be a task for the bureaucrats if it isn't a process of government resource allocation.

Funding could also be used more flexibly by those with stable long-term needs, extensive codification of permissible expenditure not being required when the overall budget has already been deemed to be reasonable and necessary. This would also help the government by enabling a shift of finite staffing resources to the more complex end, with a more hands-on role in safeguarding and specialised planning where it is most needed.

Similarly, a more strategic and active approach to market intervention, drawing on design choices from other systems that have done this rather better, could address the supply-side failings Lee identifies, but this would need careful calibration. A good place to start would be the government working together with people with disability to develop a vision of the market the NDIS needs to achieve its objectives and a plan to bring it about, including where and how the government should directly intervene.

I would like to see this go beyond addressing traditional thin markets to breaking patterns of service provision which have so far proved impervious to transformation through the individual purchasing decisions of vulnerable and isolated participants. This would include phasing out the scheme's dependence on group homes, as recommended by the Disability Royal Commission, and directly shaping a market of early intervention supports that follows the evidence and prevents participants and families being captured by providers of junk therapies.

These are some of the critical design choices ahead of us. It will be important that the government, whether steering or rowing, finds a balance in correcting major flaws in design without altering the intended destination of the NDIS as a world-leading scheme of self-directed support. They shouldn't be looking too much to the past for their reference points in doing so.

Sam Bennett

Robbi Williams

Micheline Lee's article is a valuable read for anyone new or old to the issue of disability in Australia. She charts key events leading to the advent of the NDIS, followed by a compelling narrative of the scheme's issues, punctuated by stories painful to read. It should rightly leave the reader wondering: how have we blown this so badly?

A key problem with the NDIS is it was pitched as a panacea, a nation-sized handful of magic beans growing an empowered disability community living in an inclusive Australia. However, just as the NDIS idea sat in the context of the National Disability Strategy and the United Nations Convention on the Rights of Persons with Disabilities (UNCRPD), so the decisions and actions of the NDIA, the agency administering the scheme, needed to sit in the context of a broader government push to advance inclusion policy and practice. Alas, that has not been evident. Indeed, dialogue about the progress of the first version of the National Disability Strategy, along with its sparse and tardy reporting, was entirely overshadowed by public discourse about NDIS implementation, often with a focus on where accountability lies.

First, there was the business of resolving what each government should pay. The state and territory governments scrambled to find enough extra money to pay for their share of scheme costs, and a miserable consequence was the discontinuation of some government-funded programs and mechanisms important to the disability community. Worse, because there was not enough money down the back of the sofa, the government bilateral agreements included payments-in-kind. It wasn't a watch or car keys that were pushed across the table along with cash; it was the occupants of state-run disability group homes, consigning them to even less choice than other NDIS participants. Astonishingly, funding agreements underpinning NDIS implementation included elements that preserved the types of service for which the NDIS was meant to be the antidote.

Second, there was the business of resolving which disability supports ought be scheme-funded and which ought to be covered by state and territory services in health, education, accommodation, transportation and the like. Ten years on, tensions remain at these interfaces, not least because of a default assumption that if disability is involved, it must be the responsibility of the NDIS. If you need support when admitted to hospital, the NDIS should pay. If you need support in education, the NDIS should pay. If you have accessibility needs on public transportation, the NDIS should pay. When all roads lead to the NDIS, it is little wonder this caused a stampede of diagnoses, most notably autism, so folk could be admitted into the scheme and access supports. Yet Australia's obligations to the UNCRPD mean all governments of Australia should be making far greater progress on the accessibility and inclusion of their mainstream services. It is entirely possible the manner of the NDIS's implementation has served to hinder the evolution of state and territory services towards inclusion.

This goes to a deeper issue about how our society responds to disability, where if we throw money at it – or at those who will deal with it for us – we have done our bit and can get on with our own lives. For as long as I can remember, not-for-profit disability organisations have engaged in fundraising activities to continue their work. Whether intended or not, such activities tend to portray the organisation as the hero and the disabled person as the patronised recipient. But such fundraising efforts maintain a longstanding narrative that the best way non-disabled people can contribute to the resolution of disability issues is by paying some money for someone else to take care of that business for them. On a grander scale, this is what has happened in the government's funding architecture for the NDIS implementation. If you have a disability, you go to the NDIS because that's where we've sent taxpayer money. And because of the volume of funds allocated to the NDIS, non-disabled Australians might conclude that the issue of disability is being taken of and nothing more needs to be done. But this very assumption sets up the NDIS for failure, because the NDIS needs the context of an effective disability strategy, and it is through the changed attitudes and behaviour of non-disabled Australians that we must measure the success of that strategy.

In the absence of context, the scheme's implementation made such failure even more certain through a highly transactional approach to the business of funded disability supports, coupled with a delusional level of faith in the power of the market. How could we think a market mindset would work for the NDIS? This demands not only the assumption that scheme participants are properly supported to make informed choices that miraculously shape a responsive impactful market, but also the assumption that social and economic participation can be accomplished by buying stuff. They aren't, and it can't.

Markets are transactional, whereas the NDIS is meant to be transformational. Everything about the implementation of the NDIS has felt transactional, including the calamitous sequestering of the Local Area Coordinator (LAC) role to transact scheme business instead of its intended transformational purpose of connecting people to community resources and networks. The current NDIS market is shaped by what services providers choose to offer, at prices determined by the NDIA. The NDIS participant has minimal influence in this market, and instead has become a market commodity. This is nowhere more evident than in the housing part of the NDIS – Specialist Disability Accommodation (SDA) – where private investors combine with builders and disability support providers to build shared housing that vacuums up scheme participants with the right price tag on their forehead.

So what is it we are meant to be implementing? The scheme's core values, as echoed in Micheline's essay, include "choice and control" and "social and economic participation." It follows, therefore, that the implementation ought to reflect these values. However, participant choice and control are largely absent from the current NDIS pathway, with participants having limited choice about what goes in their budgeted plan and how it might be used, and no choice of LAC. And the scheme has misunderstood the nature of social and economic participation, as revealed by the way it measures the success of this: counting the amount of time a scheme participant spends outside the home. This is not a valid measure of social participation, and at best measures physical presence in the community – a guest appearance, a very different thing from being an active and valued community member.

In addition to these core values, Lee points to the disability community's unmet expectation that the scheme would be anchored in human rights, reflecting Australia's commitment to the UNCRPD. I agree about the NDIS and the Australian Disability Strategy needing to be anchored in human rights, but ironically a narrative based on rights may not be the most effective way to win the day for an effective NDIS and an inclusive Australia. Part of the problem about the language of "rights" is that it is an intellectual discourse and can leave some people unmoved, especially those who have little or no personal experience of the issue to which the right relates. For example, there are plenty of men in Australia and elsewhere who remain disconnected from the importance of women's rights, with the result that women continue to be oppressed, overlooked or assaulted. The same is true for First Nations people. Without personal experience and insight into the issues the right speaks to, a right can become synonymous with compliance, with perceived entitlement, maybe belligerence. I am not convinced there is even a common understanding among Australians about what a right is. Rights, though critically important, are not engaging, not a crowd-pleaser, and quite possibly a turn-off.

A way through this is to see a right as a code-phrase for a collection of values. These values are held to be sufficiently important by enough people to make it worth writing them down and saying everyone should have them. By exploring the values within a right, there is a better chance of people finding a connection, be it intellectual, personal or emotional. For example, there is a right to education because of the value of education. While we might readily accept the idea of a right to education and expect people to be able to access it, we do not seem to spend much time thinking about why the right is important, about the nature of its value. That value includes, for example, the value of knowledge and skill, the value of personal development, the value of lifelong learning, the value of developing empathy and networks, the value of community, and the value of education in helping you find your place in the world.

The problem with focusing on a right rather than the values that lie within is that a right can be met transactionally. For example, a jurisdiction can meet a person's right to an education but it doesn't necessarily follow that the education so offered will be effective. But, hey, we met our obligation, we provided an education: what more do these people want, for heaven's sake? It is only by drawing out the values within a right and using those values as the explicit framework for our expectations that we can make real progress.

So what does this mean for the NDIS? It needs to move away from a transactional mindset to one that is values-driven and obsessively focused on investing in a true impact on authentic social and economic participation. That would be magnificent to see, but by itself it still won't be enough to deliver an inclusive Australia. The bigger issue lies in the broader work of all our governments. We must see more courageous and determined leadership towards inclusion. There is plenty of research data illustrating how well-crafted inclusive education is far more effective than special education at equipping young disabled people for meaningful and fulfilling adult life. Inclusive education is manifestly better at delivering the values on which the right to education is based. Yet, counterintuitively, Australia continues to invest in special and segregated education for many disabled young Australians. This also happens in other key areas of life chances, such as employment, housing, health and transportation. We need from our government and community leaders a level of determination born not just of intellectual concern at the insufficient regard for rights but of visceral outrage at the continued exclusion of disabled people from the membership and rhythms of our neighbourhoods. Despite having heard many stories of violence, abuse, neglect and exploitation, the Disability Royal Commission's recently released final report shows that commissioners were split in their view of the future of segregated mechanisms such as group housing, separate special employment and special education, and with time-lines for change to segregation that in some cases, such as education, can be measured in decades. And the report by the NDIS Quality and Safeguarding Commission earlier this year on the many instances where quality and safety have clearly been absent in group homes did not appear at any point to contemplate whether the group home model itself was fundamentally flawed. Where is the visceral outrage? Where is the manifest urgency to change things now, to dismantle these fortresses of exclusion?

To have any real chance of tackling the range of issues in Micheline Lee's essay, we must demand courageous, values-driven leadership from the governments of Australia. We must see in them visceral outrage. Let us look for this in their response to the royal commission report and to the NDIS Review report. Hold them accountable for authentic, urgent, values-driven decisions that advance inclusion now, not later.

And let each of us hold ourselves accountable for being part of the solution, not simply through donating to fundraisers or admiring the amount of taxpayer funds going to the NDIS, but by the character of our own actions, as neighbours, co-workers, employers, club members and fellow human beings.

Robbi Williams

Carly Findlay

Micheline Lee's Quarterly Essay, *Lifeboat*, is essential reading. Her story of travelling for work to Byron Writers Festival is a deeply personal one, showing her vulnerability and demonstrating that inadequate disability support compromises her independence. It disables her.

Micheline decides not to take a support worker on the way there, to save the government money – but without a support worker, and very little help from airline staff plus a flight delay, the trip turns out to be frustratingly inaccessible – and frightening. She's without her power wheelchair, which she pleads with the staff is not to be considered luggage. A flight delay means she's unable to go to the toilet for hours. It's scary, and deeply undignified – a long way from the choice and control the NDIS was designed to provide. But is the failure here just that of the NDIS or of wider society as well?

The NDIS is a difficult scheme to understand, and even more perplexing is the inconsistency in its application. It makes no sense that the NDIS will support a disabled parent to get showered and dressed, yet won't support a disabled parent to care for their baby. Just as disability can't be separated from identity, parenthood can't be separated either. Prices of mobility equipment increase if the NDIS is involved, much like the wedding tax. And getting approved for the NDIS seems to depend on the case worker you get. It makes no sense and is very unfair.

Most people I know who are on the NDIS haven't had a smooth ride. They talk about the cumbersome application process, how defeated they are to be rejected by a system that seems to know nothing about their disability, and how scary it is leading up to a plan review. The medical administration of being disabled is enormous; the NDIS adds more stressors.

The deficit model seems to be what keeps many of my disabled friends from applying. It is the main reason why I won't apply for the NDIS (or the Disability

Support Pension, either). You need to prove how disabled you are: how much you cannot do. In the case of the NDIS, disability equals inability.

Only it doesn't. Disability doesn't mean someone is unable. Disabled people have skills, hopes and dreams. And when barriers are removed, disabled people can better participate in society. And for me, disability equals pride, identity, community and culture.

The NDIS is supposed to be an investment in individuals, and Micheline writes that some plans reduce in cost with the ambitious goal of the NDIS helping people improve, making us less disabled. But many disabled people won't get "better." Many disabilities are progressive. Micheline writes of her own experience of her disability progressing, and the grief and adapting that comes with this.

In Stella Young's seminal 2014 TEDx Talk, she spoke about how disabled people don't overcome our disabilities, we overcome barriers. And these barriers aren't overcome with positive thinking, they're overcome with accessibility provisions. Stella said: "No amount of smiling at a flight of stairs has ever made it turn into a ramp. Never. Smiling at a television screen isn't going to make closed captions appear for people who are deaf. No amount of standing in the middle of a bookshop and radiating a positive attitude is going to turn all those books into braille. It's just not going to happen."

As Micheline describes, while the NDIS has helped many disabled people, there is also a misapprehension that it has solved inaccessibility across the board. Micheline has observed that people working at services such as supermarkets and airlines have stopped helping disabled people, because it's assumed that people will have a support worker. That the NDIS has "fixed" it.

The NDIS is not a catch-all. Only 480,000 Australians are on the scheme, and there are 4.5 million disabled Australians – probably more, because many disabled people don't disclose or identify. And the NDIS should not replace everyday access provisions in the community.

"I don't want the NDIS to take the focus off the need for society to be more inclusive. The NDIS has helped to minimise the individual effects of my condition. But it has not helped make society more accessible," Micheline writes. "I don't want to be confined to my own little lifeboat. I want my community to be open to all and inclusive."

So do I. The NDIS decision-making process needs to be less arbitrary and more consistent. The medical model of disability needs to be replaced with the social model of disability – where barriers are removed; and it should acknowledge that disabled people's conditions can deteriorate. As Micheline writes, there should be no shame in asking for help; the NDIS needs to be less punitive and more hopeful for participants.

Micheline Lee's Quarterly Essay should be read by every support worker, policy-maker and NDIA staff member. The NDIS must be fixed, to deliver what was promised.

Carly Findlay

Micheline Lee

Thank you to the correspondents, all experts on disability experience and/or policy, for their valuable comments on *Lifeboat*. The comments themselves are significant contributions and insights into the way forward for inclusion of disabled people and the role the NDIS should play in this. I would especially like to acknowledge the correspondence from Rhonda Galbally and the Minister for the NDIS, Bill Shorten, as they, alongside Bruce Bonyhady, were and continue to be instrumental in the development of the NDIS.

As the correspondents say, we are at a defining period for disability. The Disability Royal Commission Report and the preliminary findings of the NDIS review show that despite Australia's policies and measures to recognise disability rights, Australia has not become more inclusive. Those who are in most need of assistance continue to live at risk of abuse. In fact, under the NDIS, group home segregated living has actually increased. Galbally was a Commissioner on the Disability Royal Commission. She found that it was segregation – being "out of sight and out of mind – that enabled abuse, violence towards and neglect of disabled people. Disabled people need to be part of the community, starting from early childhood. We need structural change so that all systems – health, housing, transport, education, employment, infrastructure – are accessible and inclusive.

The NDIS was to be an important part of that structural change. We are disabled by both our bodies and by the inaccessibility of society. We need individual supports and an accessible environment in order to participate. The NDIS was to provide the individual support to those with the most significant disabilities. It was recognised that this part, though vital, was just one part of the equation. Consequently, the NDIS was originally positioned within the broader context of tiers 1 and 2, or what is now being called "the ecosystem." This was to ensure that those with less significant disabilities are supported by mainstream services, and that measures are taken to make society more accessible.

As the correspondents point out, after ten years of operation, however, the early promises of the NDIS have not been completely fulfilled. While the NDIS has benefited some, the scheme itself has been inaccessible and inequitable, particularly for some of the most disadvantaged, who need it most. And governments' focus on the NDIS has resulted in a neglect of their duties to provide support within the community and to remove social barriers.

The NDIS is revolutionary, establishing a level of entitlement to individual supports that never existed before. However, the NDIS has not increased participation, and in some ways it has resulted in society becoming less inclusive. We need to examine why, without the fear that criticising the scheme will return us to the faulty old system that we don't want repeated.

Several of the correspondents describe the problems associated with the NDIS's reliance on a classic market system. As Robbi Williams says, "How could we think a market mindset would work for the NDIS? This demands not only the assumption that scheme participants are properly supported to make informed choices that miraculously shape a responsive impactful market, but also the assumption that social and economic participation can be accomplished by buying stuff. They aren't, and it can't."

Robbi also points out how the NDIS has misunderstood what it means for disabled people to be included and participate in the community. The scheme counts participation by measuring time spent outside the home, which, he asserts, "is not a valid measure of social participation, and at best measures physical presence in the community – a guest appearance, a very different thing from being an active and valued community member."

For Carly Findlay, the NDIS doesn't reflect her lived experience of disability and of disabled people's rejection of the medical model. "In the case of the NDIS," she says, "disability equals inability." She notes the administrative burden placed on the individual by the NDIS, and that "you need to prove how disabled you are: how much you cannot do."

Member of Parliament Monique Ryan describes how the NDIS has become the "default" service and governments have defunded or removed supports in the community outside the scheme, resulting in disabled people having to be on the NDIS or get nothing. As a former paediatrician, she did as other specialists have reported doing in the absence of other available supports – she was "quicker to diagnose autism."

We all agree that to correct course, an understanding of human rights is foundational. As Bill Shorten said, "there has never been a better time in our nation's history than now to talk about the human rights of people with disability. In politics, to achieve real change, timing is everything."

The challenge is how to translate the theory of human rights into the real-life steps that will lead to the actual exercise and enjoyment of those rights by disabled people. Sam Drummond observes that, "Perhaps the greatest strength and the greatest weakness of advocating for disability rights is that everyone says they support them ... But when it comes to the crunch, will they willingly reach up to the top shelf to help us get an item? Will they support our right to lead as meaningful a life as theirs?"

Both Sam and Robbi acknowledge that, though essential, the mention of human rights can be obscure and a turn-off for many. Robbi suggests that a way through this is to "see a right as a code-phrase for a collection of values." When enough people think the values are important enough, they are written down and encapsulated within the form of a right. We can rediscover the values that are implicit within a right, and by doing that, we have "a better chance of people finding a connection, be it intellectual, personal or emotional." For example, education is valued because it brings knowledge, skill, empathy, personal development, finding your place in the world.

The difficulty people have is understanding how discrimination and disadvantage flow from society's structures. Too many people still believe these are neutral, rather than built for a narrow conception of the autonomous, white, able-bodied, middle-class human. They think that equality is about treating people the same. People don't really understand how these structures keep us shut out and how it is changing these structures and accommodating diversity that will bring inclusion.

Robbi's suggestion of emphasising the value of education and employment is important. It shows the benefits of education to the whole community and I think everyone would agree to this. But it doesn't explain that changing the narrow way education is delivered is foundational.

The No vote for the Indigenous Voice to Parliament was also a No vote for disabled people. Not just for First Nations disabled people, but for all disabled people who are disadvantaged by our narrow inaccessible structures. The struggle is in many ways shared. Waleed Aly comments that the best explanation he found for the No vote "comes from pollster Jim Reed, who concluded that Australians will vote to 'award equal opportunities to individuals regardless of their attributes,' but won't vote for something that 'treats individuals differently.'" Unlike the marriage postal vote ("equal love"), which was about treating people the same, the Voice to Parliament was about treating people differently. I agree with Waleed that in the end many Australians were unable to understand how different treatment was necessary to help achieve greater inclusion and equality.

The Convention on the Rights of Persons with Disabilities (CRPD) that came into force in 2008 was formed through active collaboration with people with disabilities from all over the world. This collaboration forged a treaty that has gone further than any other in emphasising government's responsibility to recognise structural or institutional discrimination. Just having rights was getting us nowhere – governments needed to take action to change the structures that were preventing disabled people from realising equal enjoyment of human rights.

At the heart of the CRPD is a four-dimensional understanding of equality. This conception provides a process and sets out the prerequisites for ensuring a reform or structure is likely to fulfil the right to equality. These dimensions respond to the reality of the experience of disability and disadvantage. They are not simple to understand, so I tried in *Lifeboat* to illustrate how these work through the telling of my and others' experiences of disability and the barriers to inclusion. In a nutshell, the dimensions say that you can't have inclusion without the real opportunity to pursue one's own valued choices. For that, you need to have a voice to have real negotiating power; you need real options to choose from (for example, it is not real choice if you opt for segregated education because there are no reasonable alternatives available); you need to be valued as equal and there must be recognition of your context and actual capacities; and finally, transformation of social structures to accommodate different needs is essential.

Our challenge is to find an accessible language to communicate this multidimensional approach. I see already from some of the correspondents' comments that differences can arise when it seems that we are emphasising one dimension over the other. As the CRPD emphasises, these dimensions are interdependent and all need to be satisfied.

Individual funding and the use of private providers can be beneficial; problems arise, as we have seen, when people see choice as the freedom to participate in the market without ensuring that the supports and the structures are there to allow disabled people to exercise real choice. We can't ignore the fact that people are seldom the autonomous individual born with the ability to contract and opportunities there for the taking.

The market needs to be shaped. It is government's responsibility to ensure that if it is going to use the market to deliver disability supports, then the market needs to be reformed to provide access and opportunity for all, consistent with a realistic conception of the human subject. We need a government that can counter unfettered self-interest and develop and embed the public values that are missing from the NDIS market approach.

We have seen the NDIS turning into a medical or individual model of disability support because governments have neglected broader social inclusion. Shorten calls on all governments to "commit to greater investment and effort to create inclusion: schools, transport, early childhood, community activities, advocacy, building regulations, community mental health by all levels of governments and the private sector."

As Robbi Williams says, "we must demand courageous, values-driven leadership from the governments of Australia. We must see in them visceral outrage."

When I encouraged my friend Frida to join the NDIS to get the individual supports she needed, she cried out, "I need a man." This doesn't seem so far-fetched to me if every reform such as the NDIS is treated as part of an ecosystem, and if, as Bill Shorten says, "the parts of the ecosystem are being brought together." After all, being recognised as equals, loving and being loved back is what it's all about. If Ann Marie Smith had had one friend in the world, the abuse she suffered over three years that finally took her life would not have happened.

Micheline Lee

Sam Bennett joined the Grattan Institute as its inaugural Disability Program Director in September 2023. Sam has worked on disability policy reforms for over fifteen years in Australia and the UK. In his previous role, he led the Policy, Advice and Research Division of the National Disability Insurance Agency.

Sam Drummond is a lawyer and the author of *Broke*.

Carly Findlay is a writer, speaker, appearance activist, arts worker and proud disabled woman, and the editor of *Growing Up Disabled in Australia*.

Rhonda Galbally was a board member of the National Disability Insurance Agency and Principal Member of the Independent Advisory Council, which provided advice to the NDIA. She is a commissioner of the Royal Commission into Violence, Abuse, Neglect and Exploitation of People with Disabilities.

Alan Kohler is the finance presenter on ABC News and writes for *The New Daily* and *Intelligent Investor*. A former editor of *The Age* and *The Australian Financial Review*, he founded *Eureka Report* and *Business Spectator* and has written for *The Australian*, *AFR*, *The Age* and *The Sydney Morning Herald*. His books include *It's Your Money*.

Micheline Lee's novel, *The Healing Party*, was shortlisted for several prizes, including the Victorian Premier's Literary Award. Born in Malaysia, Micheline came to Australia when she was eight. She has lived with a motor neurone disability from birth. She is a former human rights lawyer and painter.

Monique Ryan is a paediatric neurologist and politician. She is the former head of the Department of Neurology at the Royal Children's Hospital Melbourne, and the current member of parliament for the federal seat of Kooyong.

Bill Shorten is Minister for the National Disability Insurance Scheme and Minister for Government Services and a former leader of the Australian Labor Party.

Robbi Williams is the CEO of JFA Purple Orange, a social profit organisation for people with disability.

WANT THE LATEST FROM QUARTERLY ESSAY?

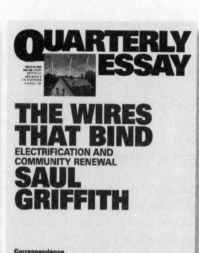

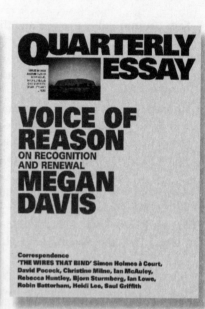

QUARTERLY ESSAY
BACK ISSUES

BACK ISSUES: (Prices include GST, postage and handling within Australia.) *Grey indicates out of stock.*

- [ ] **QE 1** ($22.99) Robert Manne *In Denial*
- [ ] **QE 2** ($22.99) John Birmingham *Appeasing Jakarta*
- [ ] **QE 3** ($22.99) Guy Rundle *The Opportunist*
- [ ] **QE 4** ($22.99) Don Watson *Rabbit Syndrome*
- [ ] **QE 5** ($22.99) Mungo MacCallum *Girt By Sea*
- [ ] **QE 6** ($22.99) John Button *Beyond Belief*
- [ ] **QE 7** ($22.99) John Martinkus *Paradise Betrayed*
- [ ] QE 8 ($22.99) Amanda Lohrey *Groundswell*
- [ ] **QE 9** ($22.99) Tim Flannery *Beautiful Lies*
- [ ] **QE 10** ($22.99) Gideon Haigh *Bad Company*
- [ ] **QE 11** ($22.99) Germaine Greer *Whitefella Jump Up*
- [ ] **QE 12** ($22.99) David Malouf *Made in England*
- [ ] **QE 13** ($22.99) Robert Manne with David Corlett *Sending Them Home*
- [ ] **QE 14** ($22.99) Paul McGeough *Mission Impossible*
- [ ] **QE 15** ($22.99) Margaret Simons *Latham's World*
- [ ] **QE 16** ($22.99) Raimond Gaita *Breach of Trust*
- [ ] **QE 17** ($22.99) John Hirst *'Kangaroo Court'*
- [ ] **QE 18** ($22.99) Gail Bell *The Worried Well*
- [ ] **QE 19** ($22.99) Judith Brett *Relaxed & Comfortable*
- [ ] **QE 20** ($22.99) John Birmingham *A Time for War*
- [ ] **QE 21** ($22.99) Clive Hamilton *What's Left?*
- [ ] **QE 22** ($22.99) Amanda Lohrey *Voting for Jesus*
- [ ] **QE 23** ($22.99) Inga Clendinnen *The History Question*
- [ ] **QE 24** ($22.99) Robyn Davidson *No Fixed Address*
- [ ] **QE 25** ($22.99) Peter Hartcher *Bipolar Nation*
- [ ] **QE 26** ($22.99) David Marr *His Master's Voice*
- [ ] **QE 27** ($22.99) Ian Lowe *Reaction Time*
- [ ] **QE 28** ($22.99) Judith Brett *Exit Right*
- [ ] **QE 29** ($22.99) Anne Manne *Love & Money*
- [ ] **QE 30** ($22.99) Paul Toohey *Last Drinks*
- [ ] **QE 31** ($22.99) Tim Flannery *Now or Never*
- [ ] **QE 32** ($22.99) Kate Jennings *American Revolution*
- [ ] **QE 33** ($22.99) Guy Pearse *Quarry Vision*
- [ ] **QE 34** ($22.99) Annabel Crabb *Stop at Nothing*
- [ ] **QE 35** ($22.99) Noel Pearson *Radical Hope*
- [ ] **QE 36** ($22.99) Mungo MacCallum *Australian Story*
- [ ] **QE 37** ($22.99) Waleed Aly *What's Right?*
- [ ] **QE 38** ($22.99) David Marr *Power Trip*
- [ ] **QE 39** ($22.99) Hugh White *Power Shift*
- [ ] **QE 40** ($22.99) George Megalogenis *Trivial Pursuit*
- [ ] **QE 41** ($22.99) David Malouf *The Happy Life*
- [ ] **QE 42** ($22.99) Judith Brett *Fair Share*
- [ ] **QE 43** ($22.99) Robert Manne *Bad News*
- [ ] **QE 44** ($22.99) Andrew Charlton *Man-Made World*
- [ ] **QE 45** ($22.99) Anna Krien *Us and Them*
- [ ] **QE 46** ($22.99) Laura Tingle *Great Expectations*
- [ ] **QE 47** ($22.99) David Marr *Political Animal*
- [ ] **QE 48** ($22.99) Tim Flannery *After the Future*
- [ ] **QE 49** ($22.99) Mark Latham *Not Dead Yet*
- [ ] **QE 50** ($22.99) Anna Goldsworthy *Unfinished Business*
- [ ] **QE 51** ($22.99) David Marr *The Prince*
- [ ] **QE 52** ($22.99) Linda Jaivin *Found in Translation*
- [ ] **QE 53** ($22.99) Paul Toohey *That Sinking Feeling*
- [ ] **QE 54** ($22.99) Andrew Charlton *Dragon's Tail*
- [ ] **QE 55** ($22.99) Noel Pearson *A Rightful Place*
- [ ] **QE 56** ($22.99) Guy Rundle *Clivosaurus*
- [ ] **QE 57** ($22.99) Karen Hitchcock *Dear Life*
- [ ] **QE 58** ($22.99) David Kilcullen *Blood Year*
- [ ] **QE 59** ($22.99) David Marr *Faction Man*
- [ ] **QE 60** ($22.99) Laura Tingle *Political Amnesia*
- [ ] **QE 61** ($22.99) George Megalogenis *Balancing Act*
- [ ] **QE 62** ($22.99) James Brown *Firing Line*
- [ ] **QE 63** ($22.99) Don Watson *Enemy Within*
- [ ] **QE 64** ($22.99) Stan Grant *The Australian Dream*
- [ ] **QE 65** ($22.99) David Marr *The White Queen*
- [ ] **QE 66** ($22.99) Anna Krien *The Long Goodbye*
- [ ] **QE 67** ($22.99) Benjamin Law *Moral Panic 101*
- [ ] **QE 68** ($22.99) Hugh White *Without America*
- [ ] **QE 69** ($22.99) Mark McKenna *Moment of Truth*
- [ ] **QE 70** ($22.99) Richard Denniss *Dead Right*
- [ ] **QE 71** ($22.99) Laura Tingle *Follow the Leader*
- [ ] **QE 72** ($22.99) Sebastian Smee *Net Loss*
- [ ] **QE 73** ($22.99) Rebecca Huntley *Australia Fair*
- [ ] **QE 74** ($22.99) Erik Jensen *The Prosperity Gospel*
- [ ] **QE 75** ($22.99) Annabel Crabb *Men at Work*
- [ ] **QE 76** ($22.99) Peter Hartcher *Red Flag*
- [ ] **QE 77** ($22.99) Margaret Simons *Cry Me a River*
- [ ] **QE 78** ($22.99) Judith Brett *The Coal Curse*
- [ ] **QE 79** ($22.99) Katharine Murphy *The End of Certainty*
- [ ] **QE 80** ($22.99) Laura Tingle *The High Road*
- [ ] **QE 81** ($22.99) Alan Finkel *Getting to Zero*
- [ ] **QE 82** ($22.99) George Megalogenis *Exit Strategy*
- [ ] **QE 83** ($22.99) Lech Blaine *Top Blokes*
- [ ] **QE 84** ($22.99) Jess Hill *The Reckoning*
- [ ] **QE 85** ($22.99) Sarah Krasnostein *Not Waving, Drowning*
- [ ] **QE 86** ($22.99) Hugh White *Sleepwalk to War*
- [ ] **QE 87** ($22.99) Waleed Aly & Scott Stephens *Uncivil Wars*
- [ ] **QE 88** ($27.99) Katharine Murphy *Lone Wolf*
- [ ] **QE 89** ($27.99) Saul Griffith *The Wires That Bind*
- [ ] **QE 90** ($27.99) Megan Davis *Voice of Reason*
- [ ] **QE 91** ($27.99) Micheline Lee *Lifeboat*

Please include this form with delivery and payment details overleaf.
Back issues also available as ebooks from ebook retailers

SUBSCRIBE TO RECEIVE NEARLY 20% OFF THE COVER PRICE

☐ **ONE-YEAR PRINT AND DIGITAL SUBSCRIPTION: $89.99**

- Print edition
- Home delivery
- Automatically renewing
- Full digital access to all past issues
- App for Android and iPhone users
- ebook files

DELIVERY AND PAYMENT DETAILS

DELIVERY DETAILS:

NAME:

ADDRESS:

EMAIL: _____ PHONE:

PAYMENT DETAILS: Enclose a cheque/money order made out to Schwartz Books Pty Ltd.
Or debit my credit card (MasterCard, Visa and Amex accepted).
Freepost: Quarterly Essay, Reply Paid 90094, Collingwood VIC 3066
All prices include GST, postage and handling.

CARD NO. ☐☐☐☐ ☐☐☐☐ ☐☐☐☐ ☐☐☐☐ ☐☐☐☐

EXPIRY DATE: ____ / ____ CCV: ____ AMOUNT: $ ____

PURCHASER'S NAME: _____ SIGNATURE:

Subscribe online at **quarterlyessay.com/subscribe** • Freecall: 1800 077 514 • Phone: 03 9486 0288
Email: subscribe@quarterlyessay.com (please do not send electronic scans of this form)